SCHOLASTIC

Teaching
Reading & Writing
With Nursery Rhymes

BY DEBORAH SCHECTER

NEW YORK • TORONTO • LONDON • AUCKLAND • SYDNEY
MEXICO CITY • NEW DELHI • HONG KONG • BUENOS AIRES

Teaching *Resources*

for David.

Special thanks to Joan Novelli and Mackie Rhodes for their invaluable suggestions.

Cover design by Jason Robinson
Interior design by Kathy Massaro
Interior illustrations by Maxie Chambliss

ISBN-13: 978-0-439-15585-4
ISBN-10: 0-439-15585-1

Copyright © 2008 by Deborah Schecter
Published by Scholastic Inc.
All rights reserved.
Printed in the U.S.A.

1 2 3 4 5 6 7 8 9 10   40   15 14 13 12 11 10 09 08

Contents

About This Book 4

Connections to the Language Arts Standards 5

Teaching With the Rhymes 6

Extending the Lessons 9

References and Resources 15

My Nursery Rhyme Read-and-Write Sheet 16

PHONICS & WORD WORK

Bow-Wow (initial consonants) 17

Little Jack Horner (consonant blends and digraphs) 25

Baa, Baa, Black Sheep (short and long vowels) 31

Little Bo-Peep (short- and long-vowel phonograms) 36

The Old Woman Who Lived in a Shoe (sight words) 46

Little Boy Blue (word building) 53

The Itsy Bitsy Spider (word building) 60

VOCABULARY

Jack and Jill (action words) 68

Hey, Diddle, Diddle (positional words and phrases) 75

The Queen of Hearts (shape words) 82

Pease Porridge Hot (opposites) 90

Roses Are Red (color words) 96

Mrs. Hen (number and color words) 103

READING COMPREHENSION & WRITING

Humpty Dumpty (summarizing and retelling; problems and solutions) 110

Blow, Wind, Blow (sequencing) 115

Little Miss Muffet (point of view) 124

Three Little Kittens (descriptive language) 131

Old Mother Hubbard (fluency) 138

About This Book

What the Research Says

▲▲▲▲▲▲▲

MacLean, Bryant, and Bradley (1987) found that there is a strong relationship between young children's familiarity with nursery rhymes, their phonological development, and their future success in reading and spelling.

Jack and Jill

Jack and Jill went up the hill
to fetch a pail of water.
Jack fell down and broke his crown,
and Jill came tumbling after.

Teaching Tip

▲▲▲▲▲▲▲

Enlarge the patterns when photocopying, using cardstock or heavyweight paper. Or glue the patterns to cardboard. Laminate for durability.

Beloved nursery rhymes such as "Jack and Jill," "Hey, Diddle, Diddle," and "Little Miss Muffet" have been cherished by children for generations. Their rhyme, repetition, predictability—and often their silliness—make them fun and appealing for children to listen to and recite. Nursery rhymes naturally lend themselves to phonemic awareness and phonics work as well as a multitude of other teaching opportunities. This book features 18 nursery rhymes that let children revisit favorite classics and get acquainted with rhymes they may not know.

Each of the featured rhymes contains a focus lesson in one of three main categories: phonics and word work, vocabulary, and reading comprehension and writing. The lessons also include ideas that target the other categories as well as connections to math, social studies, and science. And to support brain research indicating that children who involve multiple modalities in learning are better able to acquire, retain, and remember what they learn, you'll find ideas for incorporating drama, movement, singing, art, and manipulatives. The lesson for each rhyme includes the following features:

⭐ **Nursery Rhyme** Each rhyme appears on its own ready-to-reproduce page. Large, easy-to-read print and illustrations that closely match the text support beginning readers.

⭐ **Concepts & Skills** See at a glance the focus concepts and skills of a lesson.

⭐ **Materials** Use this handy list to gather the materials needed for each lesson.

⭐ **Getting Ready** Set-up instructions, easy how-to's, and helpful tips ensure that activities go smoothly.

⭐ **Reading the Rhyme** These ideas, strategies, and mini-lessons help you use the nursery rhyme to teach different concepts and skills.

⭐ **Introducing the Activity** Give children further practice with the lesson's target concepts and skills with engaging activities, games, and manipulatives. Most include patterns that are ready to photocopy. Step-by-step how-to's guide you in introducing activities to children. Use the activities with the whole class, in small groups, or in a learning center for independent practice.

Jack and Jill

hop

up the hill.

⭐ **Focus On . . . Extension Activities** These extension activities offer opportunities to reinforce the concepts and skills of the lesson, and more.

Connections to the Language Arts Standards

The featured poems, lessons, and activities in this book support the following K-1 standards outlined by Mid-continent Research for Education and Learning (McREL), an organization that collects and synthesizes national and state K–12 curriculum standards.

Reading

- Understands how print is organized and read
- Uses mental images based on pictures and print to aid in comprehension of text
- Uses meaning clues to aid comprehension and make predictions about content
- Uses phonetic and structural analysis to decode unknown words
- Understands level-appropriate sight words and vocabulary
- Reads aloud familiar poems with fluency and expression
- Knows main ideas or theme, setting, main characters, main events, sequence, and problems in stories
- Summarizes information found in texts (retells in own words)
- Makes simple inferences regarding the order of events and possible outcomes
- Relates stories to personal experiences

Writing

- Uses strategies to organize written work
- Uses writing and other methods to describe familiar persons, places, objects, or experiences
- Writes for different purposes and in a variety of forms or genres
- Uses descriptive words to convey basic ideas, and declarative and interrogative sentences in written work
- Uses conventions of print in writing
- Applies beginning knowledge of grammar rules
- Uses phonics knowledge and conventions of spelling in written work (spells high-frequency words; uses letter-sound relationships; uses resources to spell words (word walls)

Support for English Language Learners

▲ ▲ ▲ ▲ ▲ ▲

In their book *English Language Learners: The Essential Guide* (Scholastic, 2007), authors David Freeman and Yvonne Freeman encourage the use of nursery rhymes with English language learners. The characteristics of nursery rhymes that make them so useful in teaching young children to read also support children who are learning a second language. Authentic texts that follow certain patterns (repetitive, cumulative), and include devices such as rhyme, rhythm, and alliteration, make text easier to predict and offer support for meaning construction. The lessons that accompany the rhymes in this book also include opportunities to use visuals such as props, puppets, dramatic play, and hands-on manipulatives that help make language and concepts more tangible for English language learners.

▲▲▲▲▲▲

It's helpful to point out specific words and track print as you read the rhymes. Fanciful reading wands enhance the experience! For "The Queen of Hearts," for example, hot-glue a sparkly pipe-cleaner heart to a dowel; for "The Itsy Bitsy Spider," use a wiggly plastic spider!

Check the following books, CDs, and Web sites for traditional nursery rhyme melodies:

◆ Bus Songs
www.bussongs.com/songs/

◆ Just Playing: Nursery Rhymes and Other Silly Stuff
www.smart-central.com

◆ Nicky's Nursery Rhymes
www.nurseryrhymes4u.com

◆ *Teaching Tunes Audio CD and Mini-Books Set: Nursery Rhymes* (Scholastic, 2002)

◆ *Wee Sing Nursery Rhymes and Lullabies Gift Set*, Books and CDs (Price Stern Sloan, 2007; reissue)

Teaching With the Rhymes

To enrich children's reading experiences, use the following suggestions and strategies with any of the nursery rhymes in this book.

Before Reading

Use these tips to prepare for the lessons and ensure that they go smoothly:

Setting Up

⭐ Create enlarged versions of the rhymes to use for shared reading. Write the rhymes on chart paper or write each line on separate sentence strips for use in a pocket chart. (Specific set-up suggestions appear in each lesson.)

⭐ Laminate the rhymes so that they can be written on and reused. Use wipe-off markers to highlight particular words or spelling patterns.

⭐ Alternately, you might copy the poetry pages onto transparencies for use on an overhead projector during shared reading. This option allows children to see the illustrations that support the text.

Introducing the Rhymes

Since most nursery rhymes were written hundreds of years ago, many contain words that are not in use today. So it's important to provide background information for any words or concepts that might be unfamiliar to children.

During Reading

Support children in their reading efforts and help them develop useful reading strategies with these suggestions:

⭐ Model good reading techniques such as reading from left to right and crossing the text with a steady, sweeping eye movement.

⭐ After reading aloud a rhyme a few times, ask children to join in for a shared reading. Invite children to tap the rhythmic beat by clapping their hands or drumming the floor.

⭐ Discuss strategies for decoding unfamiliar words, such as finding beginning or ending sounds, breaking the word into parts, and using picture clues.

⭐ Point out punctuation, capital letters, and other conventions of print.

⭐ Share the traditional melodies of different nursery rhymes (or make up your own). This helps children build phonemic awareness, recognize rhyming patterns, and develop intonation and phrasing.

After Reading

Help children reflect on what they have read, reinforce skills and concepts, and extend learning with the following ideas:

⭐ Ask children what they liked most and least about a particular rhyme. To assess comprehension, have children do an oral retelling. See Summarize and Retell (page 12) for more.

⭐ Since many nursery rhymes contain children's names, for example, "Little Jack Horner" and "Little Bo-Peep," substitute children's names using self-sticking notes.

⭐ Innovate on a rhyme by substituting real or nonsense rhyming words, as in the examples to the right:

> Humpty Dumpty wanted to rest.
> So Humpty Dumpty sat on a nest.
>
> Humpty Dumpty was very, very late.
> So Humpty Dumpty decided to skate!

Using the Reproducible Nursery Rhyme Pages

Once children are very familiar with a rhyme through shared reading, give them a copy of the nursery rhyme page to use for independent reading (or singing!) and for reading to classmates or family members. You might also use copies of the rhymes to help children focus on specific skills. For example:

Little Bo-Peep

Little Bo-Peep
has lost her sheep,
and doesn't know where to find them.
Leave them alone, and they'll come home,
wagging their tails behind them.

⭐ Have children underline or highlight the rhyming words or sight words.

⭐ Mask the sight words or rhyming words in a poem and ask children to fill in the missing words. In "Little Bo-Peep" (page 36), for example, you might omit *sheep* from the first line and ask children to fill in other words that rhyme with *sheep*. (Enlarged copies of the poetry pages work well for this exercise.)

⭐ Cut a poem into strips, one line per strip. Mix them up for children to reorder. See Strengthen Sequencing Skills (page 8) for more.

⭐ To monitor children's decoding skills, take a running record as they read a poetry page independently, noting the problem-solving strategies used by each child as well as strengths and needs.

⭐ Have children make a collection of the poetry pages. Provide 11- by 17-inch sheets of construction paper, folded in half. Let children decorate the cover of their book and title it "My Nursery Rhyme Book." They can then insert the poems and bind.

Building Skills With Pocket Charts

A pocket chart is a useful and flexible tool to use with nursery rhymes. Write each line of a rhyme on a separate sentence strip and place in the pockets. Then try these suggestions:

⭐ **Work on Word Recognition** On index cards, draw pictures or use stickers or pictures from old workbooks to illustrate particular words in a rhyme. As children read the poem aloud with you, invite volunteers to come up to the pocket chart and place each picture beside the word it illustrates.

⭐ **Reinforce Rhyming** Cut off the rhyming words from the sentence strips. Place these at the bottom of the pocket chart. Encourage children to replace the missing words, using sounds and spelling patterns as clues.

⭐ **Create Cloze Activities**

When preparing the sentence strips for a rhyme, replace one or two words with blank lines. Then cut a blank sentence strip to fit the space left by each blank, and write the missing word on the strip. Hand out the word strips, and then read aloud the rhyme. When you come to a blank ask, "Who has the word that will complete this line?" Let the child with that word insert it over the blank line. Together, reread the line to see if it makes sense. Repeat this process for each missing word.

⭐ **Strengthen Sequencing Skills** Once children are familiar with a particular rhyme, place the sentence strips randomly in the pockets so that the rhyme is out of order. Invite children to help you put the lines in correct sequence, encouraging them to use sequencing vocabulary, such as *first, second, third,* and *last.* As an added challenge, cut a sentence strip into individual words and have children reorder the phrase or sentence, or slot in new words. After a lesson, put the set of strips in a center for children to use independently or in pairs. Number them on the back for self-checking.

Teaching Tips

▲▲▲▲▲▲

◆ To introduce children to sequencing, ask them to draw a picture to illustrate each line of a nursery rhyme. Then have them mix up the pictures and put them in the correct order.

◆ For lessons that focus on sequencing, see "The Itsy Bitsy Spider" (page 60) and "Blow, Wind, Blow (page 115).

Extending the Lessons

This book has been organized into three main categories: phonics and word work, vocabulary, and reading comprehension and writing. On pages 9–15, you'll find ideas to reinforce and extend the lessons in each category as well as for the rhymes and lessons in other parts of the book.

Phonics & Word Work

The musical rhythms and predictability of nursery rhymes make them perfect for helping children focus on different phonics skills.

Chant and Clap

Once children are familiar with a particular poem, ask them to chant the words as they clap out the syllables in each line. This will help them segment the words and hear the different phonemes that make up each word.

Spelling Patterns

Invite children to listen for the rhymes in the poem. For example, ask children to listen and clap for *moon* and *spoon* in "Hey, Diddle, Diddle" (page 75), and *blue* and *you* in "Roses Are Red" (page 96). Guide children to notice that rhyming words can have similar and different spelling patterns. During a rereading, invite children to use the predictability of the text to anticipate and predict the rhymes in upcoming lines.

Sound-Letter Correspondence

Tell children to listen for words that begin with a particular consonant, blend or digraph, or contain a certain vowel sound. For example, have them clap whenever they hear a word in "The Itsy Bitsy Spider" (page 60) that begins with the *sp* sound (*spider, spout*). Ask: "What other words do you know that begin with this sound?"

Word Sorts

After reading a rhyme, follow up by preparing word cards labeled with words from the rhyme that you wish to target and review. Have children sort the words in different ways: words with two/three letters; words that rhyme/don't rhyme; long/short vowel words, and so on. Also invite children to come up with their own ways to sort and then explain the basis for the groups they made.

Word Building

Follow up the word work activities in the lessons for "Little Boy Blue" (page 53), and "The Itsy Bitsy Spider" (page 60) by having children use the letter tiles (page 59) to practice word building. Children can mix up the letters for a given word and then reform it. They can also use the letter tiles to segment and then blend the sounds in certain words.

A Note About Sight Words

▲ ▲ ▲ ▲ ▲ ▲

Encourage children to keep an eye out for sight words that appear in the poems, such as *of*, *and*, and *the*. Accurate and automatic recognition of these high-frequency words enables children to read more smoothly and at a faster rate, helping them remember more of what they have just read and to make sense of it. The nursery rhymes in this book contain more than 100 words from the Dolch Basic Sight Vocabulary. Originally formulated by E.W. Dolch in 1941, the 220 words on this list still comprise more than 50% of the words primary-age children encounter most frequently in the print materials they use (Johns, 1976 as cited in Blevins, 2006). For a lesson that specifically focuses on sight words, see "The Old Woman Who Lived in a Shoe" (page 46).

What the Research Says

▲▲▲▲▲▲

Beck, McKeown & Kucan (2002) have found that explicit instruction in vocabulary as well as repeated encounters with new words are critical in helping children develop a deep knowledge of word meanings. Their research also highlights the importance of introducing children to rich, colorful words to help them develop a wide, mature vocabulary.

Teaching Tip

▲▲▲▲▲▲

Before making a map for a newly learned word, give children practice in mapping a word they know, such as *dog* or *flower*.

Vocabulary

Suggested strategies and ideas for helping young children expand and deepen their vocabulary follow.

Model With Think Alouds

During a shared reading, pause when you encounter an unfamiliar word or difficult concept. For example, while reading "Little Miss Muffet," you might stop at the word *tuffet* and model how to use context clues to figure out its meaning. (See page 125.) The word *fetch* in "Jack and Jill" can set the stage for a mini-lesson on synonyms. (See page 69.)

Make Word Walls

Display key vocabulary from the rhymes or related topics. After reading "The Itsy Bitsy Spider" (page 60), you might make a word wall of weather words. Let children help display and organize the words. Simply write the words on tagboard strips or use any of the patterns from this book. Add supportive pictures, if desired. Use removable adhesive to attach them to the wall at children's eye level (this allows children to take the words down for use at their desk and then return them to the wall.) Refer to the word wall frequently and encourage children to use it during independent writing. (For excellent, interactive word wall activities, see *Teaching Reading and Writing With Word Walls* by Janiel M. Wagstaff [Scholastic, 1999].)

Use Graphic Organizers

Introduce unfamiliar words or reinforce new vocabulary using graphic organizers. A concept or word map (Schwartz and Raphael, 1985) is a useful organizer for helping children deeply process new words. For example, after discussing the meaning of the word *porridge* in "Pease Porridge Hot" (page 90), you might guide children to fill in an organizer like the one shown here:

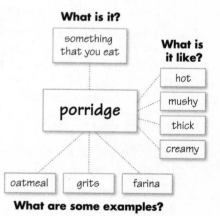

Categorize and Find Relationships Between Words

To deepen vocabulary, it's important to teach concepts and words together, and to help children connect new words to concepts they already know (Beck, McKeown & Kucan, 2002). Have children work collaboratively to sort and classify or compare and contrast words. In the lesson for "Little Boy Blue" for example, children categorize farm-related words. (See page 56.) For "Pease, Porridge Hot," they broaden their vocabulary by working with words that describe the continuum between the opposites, *hot* and *cold*. (See page 93.)

Reading Comprehension

Despite their brevity, nursery rhymes tell simple stories. This makes them just right for introducing the elements of story structure and comprehension strategies.

Identify Story Elements

After reading "Jack and Jill" (page 68) you might help children identify main characters, setting, plot, and problems and resolutions by asking:

⭐ Who is the poem about?

⭐ Where does the poem take place?

⭐ What were Jack and Jill doing?

⭐ What happened?

Mix-and-Match Nursery Rhymes

Invite children to explore story elements and have fun innovating on the rhymes. On separate slips of paper, write the names of different nursery rhyme characters, settings, and problems. Label a bag for each category and place the slips of paper in their corresponding bags. Have three volunteers each choose a slip from one of the bags and read it aloud. As a class, use the examples to make up a story (serious or silly). Then divide the class into groups of three and repeat the activity, challenging each group to use their choices to come up with a story to tell the rest of the class.

Predict Outcomes

"Old Mother Hubbard went to the cupboard..." When reading a rhyme that is unfamiliar to children, stop after the first line (or first few lines) and ask: "What do you think might happen next?" Then read the rest of the rhyme and have children compare their predictions with what actually takes place.

Recognize Cause and Effect

Many nursery rhymes offer opportunities to explore cause and effect. The events that occur are simple and the effects immediate and very clear. In "Humpty Dumpty" for example, the cause was falling off a wall. The effect? He broke into pieces and couldn't be mended. Using the rhymes to explore cause and effect will provide a foundation for a more complex understanding of this strategy later on in school.

Real or Fantasy?

Nursery rhyme characters such as cows and sheep are real animals. But can a cow really jump over the moon? Does a sheep have wool? Use the rhymes to help children distinguish between realism and fantasy.

Compare and Contrast

Create a chart such as the one shown here to help children compare and contrast the features of different rhymes.

Nursery Rhyme Feature	Little Boy Blue	Baa, Baa, Black Sheep	Little Bo-Peep	Little Miss Muffet
children	✳	✳	✳	✳
chores/jobs	✳	✳	✳	
animals	✳	✳	✳	✳
talking animals		✳		
food				✳

Teaching Tip

▲▲▲▲▲▲▲

Before using retellings to assess comprehension, model the skill and give children ample practice time.

Summarize and Retell

Inviting children to retell a nursery rhyme can indicate what they recall, their understanding of story structure, and how well they organize, sequence, and make connections to what they have read or heard. In addition to retelling orally, children might retell a rhyme in pictures and/or writing. Punch two holes along one edge of several sheets of construction paper. Have children retell the rhyme (individually or in groups) by illustrating on separate sheets the key events of the story and adding words, as desired. Have children string the pictures in order, through a length of yarn, and then share their retelling with the class.

Make Text Connections

A key component of comprehension is the ability of readers to connect what they have read to their own lives, to other texts they have read, and to the world in which they live. A chart is a simple yet effective tool for helping children practice making such connections. For example:

Three Little Kittens	This rhyme made me feel... (text-to-self)	This rhyme reminded me of... (text-to-text)	This rhyme made me think about... (text-to-world)
◆ They lost their mittens and cried.	◆ I felt really sad when my favorite flip-flops got lost.	◆ Little Bo-Peep, because she lost her sheep.	◆ If you lose something, you can look in the Lost and Found.

Draw Conclusions and Make Inferences

To help children reflect on the rhymes, ask questions such as:

⭐ Why do you think that happened?

⭐ Why did the character(s) do that?"

⭐ Would you like to know more about [sheep, spiders, windmills]?

Build Fluency

The length and natural rhythm of nursery rhymes make them well suited for fluency practice, a critical component of reading comprehension.

⭐ **Punctuation and Phrasing** Nursery rhymes often contain a range of punctuation and phrasing, two key elements of fluency. For example, the line-by-line arrangement of meaningful chunks of text gives children cues about phrase boundaries. As you read aloud the rhymes, model good reading behaviors by pointing out ways in which pacing, expression, punctuation, and inflection provide meaning clues. For example:

  ● To show how punctuation affects inflection, read aloud part of a rhyme using somewhat exaggerated expression. Repeat the demonstration and then ask children to read aloud with you.

  ● After reading "Where is the young boy who looks after the sheep?" in "Little Boy Blue" (page 53), guide children to notice the question mark at the end of the sentence and how it affects the meaning.

  ● Use rhymes that include dialogue, such as "Bow-Wow" (page 17), "Baa, Baa, Black Sheep" (page 31), and "Three Little Kittens" (page 131) to model changing inflection and using distinct voices for different speakers.

⭐ **Choral and Echo Reading** Choral reading (in which the teacher and children read together as a group) encourages children to read at the same pace and with the same phrasing and intonation as the rest of the group. This approach works especially well with nursery rhymes because of their distinct patterns. In echo reading, you read a line and children then repeat it, echoing your expression, tone, and pacing. You might also make audiotapes of different rhymes that include pauses in which children can echo the reading.

⭐ **Repeated Readings** The brief, predictable nature of nursery rhymes make them perfect for repeated reading, another component in building fluency (Rasinski, 2003). Have children read and reread a rhyme many times to become very familiar with the text. Once decoding is no longer the emphasis, the child can focus more on comprehension. Let children practice repeated readings independently, in pairs, or by taking the rhyme home to read to family members or even a pet!

What the Research Says

▲▲▲▲▲▲

"Reading fluency refers to the ability of readers to read quickly, effortlessly, and efficiently with good, meaningful expression." (Rasinski, 2003, p. 26)

Teaching Tip

▲▲▲▲▲▲

For lessons that focus on fluency, see "Bow-Wow" (page 17), "The Old Woman Who Lived in a Shoe" (page 46), "Three Little Kittens" (page 131), and "Old Mother Hubbard" (page 138).

My Nursery Rhyme Read-and-Write Sheet

▲▲▲▲▲▲

Use the record sheet on page 16 with any of the activities in this book. The page provides a place for children to practice spelling and writing the words, phrases, or sentences they are learning. The record sheet also offers you a way to track children's writing progress.

Writing

Motivate your budding writers by stocking a writing center with a variety of writing tools and colored paper. Suggested writing activities to use with the rhymes follow.

The Further Adventures of . . .

Invite children to write a poem (it doesn't have to rhyme) or story about the further adventures of favorite nursery rhyme characters. Offer prompts, such as "Where do you think the dish and the spoon were going at the end of 'Hey, Diddle, Diddle?' Who did they meet?" Children might write and illustrate their tale as a storyboard for classmates to screen like a movie.

Nursery Rhyme Pair-Ups

What if the Three Little Kittens spent a day with Old Mother Hubbard's dog? Or Jack and Jill met up with Humpty Dumpty? What kinds of situations or problems might result from such pairings? Let children pair up to write a short skit to present to the class. Have each child choose a nursery rhyme character to include in the skit. Before they write, encourage children to compare and contrast the characters and the rhymes in which they appear.

Nursery Rhymes in the News

Create a class newspaper titled "Nursery Rhyme Times" and include stories children write about their favorites. Teach children about using some or all of the five *w*'s (*who*, *what*, *where*, *when*, and *why*) in their stories. To plan what they will write, have them use pictures or words to fill in a simple graphic organizer, like the one below:

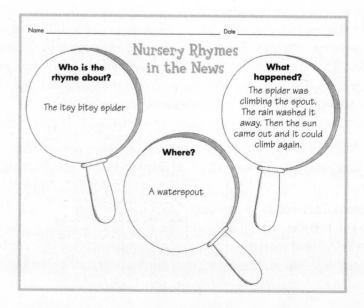

Who Am I? Nursery Rhyme Riddles

Challenge children to write riddles about nursery rhyme characters and read them to classmates. This exercise also helps assess their recall of main idea and details.

I was having breakfast.
A spider came.
I got scared away.

Who am I? (*Miss Muffet*)

Assessing Writing

Create simple rubrics and checklists, including self-assessments (similar to the one shown at right), to track children's progress in writing.

Name _____ Date _____

My Writing Checklist

	Yes	No
I put spaces between words.	☐	☐
I used capital letters to begin sentences.	☐	☐
I used capital letters to begin names.	☐	☐
Each sentence ends with a punctuation mark (. ! ?)	☐	☐

References and Resources

Bear, D. R., Invernizzi, M., Templeton, S. R., & Johnston, F. (2000). *Words Their Way: Word Study for Phonics, Vocabulary, and Spelling Instruction* (2nd ed.). Upper Saddle River, NJ: Prentice Hall.

Beck, I. L., McKeown, M. G., & Kucan, L. (2002). *Bringing Words to Life: Robust Vocabulary Instruction*. New York: The Guilford Press.

Blevins, W. (2001). *Building Fluency: Lessons and Strategies for Reading Success*. New York: Scholastic.

Blevins, W. (2006). *Phonics From A to Z: A Practical Guide* (2nd ed.). New York: Scholastic.

Fiderer, A. (1998). *35 Rubrics & Checklists to Assess Reading and Writing*. New York: Scholastic.

Franzese, R. (2002). *Reading and Writing in Kindergarten*. New York: Scholastic.

Freeman, D., & Freeman, Y. (2007). *English Language Learners: The Essential Guide*. New York: Scholastic.

Goswami, U. (2001). Early phonological development and the acquisition of literacy. In S. B. Neuman & D. K. Dickinson (Eds.), *Handbook of Early Literacy Research* (pp. 111–125). New York: The Guilford Press.

Kendall, J. S., & Marzano, R. J. (2004). *Content knowledge: A compendium of standards and benchmarks for K—12 education* (4th ed.). Aurora, CO: Mid-Continent Research for Education and Learning. Online database: http://www.mcrel.org/standards-benchmarks/

MacLean, M., Bryant P., & Bradley, L. (1987). Rhymes, nursery rhymes, and reading in early childhood. *Merrill-Palmer Quarterly, 33* (3), 255–281.

Moore, P., & Lyon A. (2005). *New Essentials for Teaching Reading in PreK—2*. New York: Scholastic.

Rasinski, T. V. (2003). *The Fluent Reader*. New York: Scholastic.

Schwartz, R. M., & Raphael, T. E. (1985). Concept of definition: A key to improving students' vocabulary. *Reading Teacher, 39.* 198–203.

Wagstaff, J. M. (1999). *20 Weekly Word Study Poetry Packets*. New York: Scholastic.

Name _____ Date _____

My Nursery Rhyme
Read-and-Write Sheet

_____

_____

_____

_____

_____

_____

_____

_____

_____

_____

Bow-Wow

"Bow-wow," says the dog.
"Meow-meow," says the cat.
"Grunt-grunt," says the hog,
and "squeak," goes the rat.
"Buzz-buzz," says the bee.
"Tweet-tweet," says the jay.
"Caw-caw," says the crow.
"Quack-quack," says the duck.
And what the cuckoo says, you know!

Bow-Wow

Teaching Tip

▲ ▲ ▲ ▲ ▲ ▲

◆ In the rhyme, the words *grunt* and *tweet* begin with consonant blends. Depending on your instructional goals, you may choose to introduce these to children or simply limit the discussion to the initial letter of each word in this rhyme.

Getting Ready

1. Write the poem (page 17) on chart paper, on sentence strips and place in a pocket chart, or copy it onto a transparency.

2. Write a list of the consonants on chart paper or a whiteboard.

3. See page 7 for suggested ways to use the poetry page with your class.

Reading the Rhyme

1. Read aloud the rhyme, and then invite children to take turns reading aloud each line. As they say each animal's part, encourage children to use lots of expression to make the sound as the animal might.

2. Tell children that you're going to read the poem again. Have them listen and look carefully for animal-sound words or animal names that begin with consonant letters.

3. As you reread the rhyme, emphasize words with initial consonants. After reading, let children take turns using a marker to underline the initial consonants in the poem. Encourage them to read aloud each word, emphasizing the beginning consonant sound.

4. Ask children: "What if these animals could really talk? What might they say?" As children share their ideas, record them on chart paper. Encourage children to use words that begin with the same consonant as the animal names—for example, "I like doughnuts," says the dog, or "Hello," says the hog. (Pair this activity with Focus On . . . Fluency, page 20, to reinforce conventions of dialogue.)

Animal Talk Book

This mini-book activity gives children more practice with initial consonants.

Getting Ready

Copy a set of mini-book pages for each child.

Introducing the Activity

1. Give each child a set of mini-book pages. Have children cut them apart. Ask them to look at the picture on the cover. Then read aloud the title. Ask, "What do you think this book will be about?"

2. Explain that in this book the animals talk! Review pages 1–7, pointing out the speech bubble near each animal's mouth. Explain that a speech bubble is a signal to readers that a character is talking. Point out the sentence beneath each animal. Explain the use of quotation marks as another way to show that a character is speaking. (See Focus On . . . Fluency, page 20, for more.) Tell children that they will write the word each animal says in the speech bubble and in the sentence.

3. Together, review each page. Read aloud the animal's name and invite children to name the consonant that begins the name. Explain that the word each animal says should begin with the same letter and sound as the animal's name. Demonstrate by completing page 1 together. First, name the animal (*dog*). Then read the words in the Word Bank on page 7 and do a think aloud: "Which word would the dog say? *Come, jump, bow . . . dig . . .* It's *dig*, because *dig* begins with /d/, the same sound at the beginning of *dog*."

4. Model how to write the word *dig* in the speech bubble and the sentence frame. Conclude by asking children what they notice about the words *dog* and *dig*. (*They both begin with the same sound and letter.*)

5. Revisit the words in the Word Bank and review the sound and letter that begins each word. Then have children complete pages 2–6. When finished, help them place all of the pages in order (including the cover and page 7). Then help them staple along the left side to bind.

6. Have children take turns with a partner reading aloud their books. Encourage them to read with expression, as they think the animals might sound if they could talk.

(continues)

★ mini-book page patterns (pages 21–24)

★ crayons, colored pencils, or markers

★ scissors

★ stapler

Teaching Tip

For a more challenging activity, mask the Word Bank on mini-book page 7 before photocopying. Invite children to fill in words of their choosing that begin with the same letter as each animal's name.

19

"Kick," says the kangaroo.

7. As an extension, invite children to think of an animal name that begins with a different consonant than the ones in the book—for example, *fish, lion, kangaroo, mouse, tiger*. On a separate sheet of paper, tell children to draw that animal, fill in a speech bubble to show what it says, and then copy and fill in a sentence frame like the ones in the mini-book. Compile children's pages into a class book they will enjoy reading again and again.

Focus On . . .

Phonics: Rhyming Words

To help children explore the rhyming words in this poem, have them make new books in which the animals from the poem say things that rhyme with their names, as in the example to the right:

> "I like to jog," says the dog.
> "I want a bat," says the cat.
> "Look at the log," says the hog.
> "I like that tree," says the bee.
> "That is my hat," says the rat.
> "Good day," says the jay.
> "I like to row," says the crow.
> "Just my luck," says the duck.

Vocabulary: Animal Names and Sounds

Share with children books about animals to help them learn other animal names. For extra fun, explore onomatopoeia (words that mimic the sound they describe) by inviting children to take turns making the sounds of different animals. Classmates can try to guess the animal that makes each sound. On chart paper or a whiteboard, list the animals and the sounds they make. Invite children to use the list to create innovations on the nursery rhyme.

Fluency: Expression and Dialogue

Ask children how they know the animals in the poem are speaking. (*The sentences include the speaker tag* says *and quotation marks around the words the animals say.*) Invite children to look for and share examples of dialogue and speaker tags in poems and stories they read.

Teaching Tip

▲ ▲ ▲ ▲ ▲

For English-language speakers in the United States, ducks "quack." But did you know that Pakistani ducks go "tay-tay-tay" and Japanese ducks go "da-da-da?" Invite children from other cultures in your class to share animal sounds in their native language. You can also take a virtual field trip to barnyards around the world by visiting www.bzzzpeek.com to hear how children in different countries make the sounds for different animals.

"_____"

says the dog.

Teaching Reading & Writing With Nursery Rhymes © 2008 by Deborah Schecter, Scholastic Teaching Resources

My Animal Talk Book

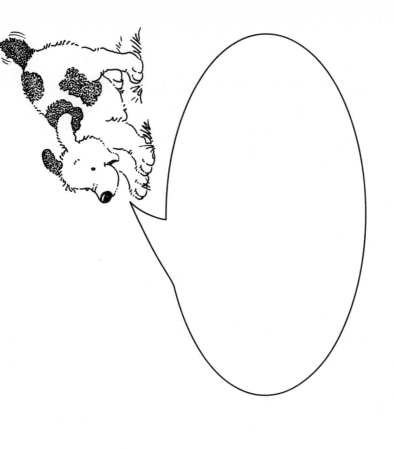

By _____

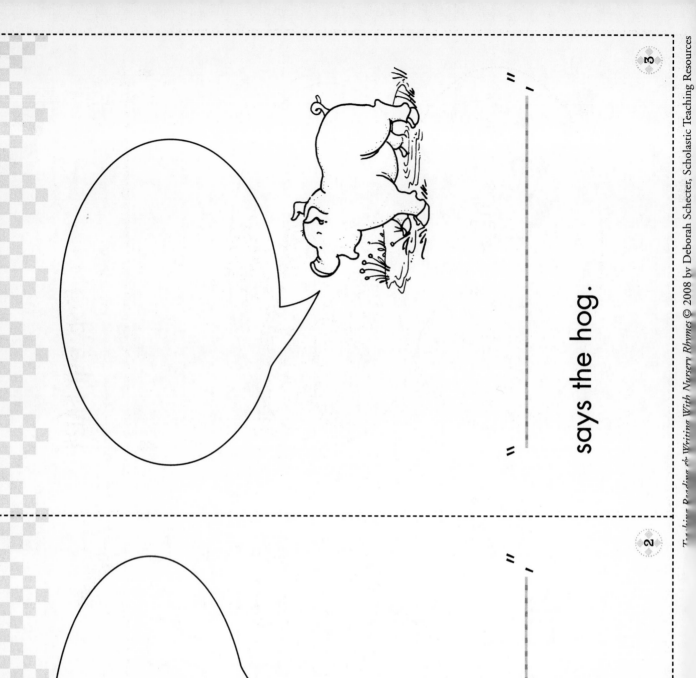

"_____,"

says the hog.

③

"_____,"

says the cat.

②

Teaching Reading & Writing With Nursery Rhymes © 2008 by Deborah Schecter, Scholastic Teaching Resources

"_____"

says the jay.

"_____"

says the bee.

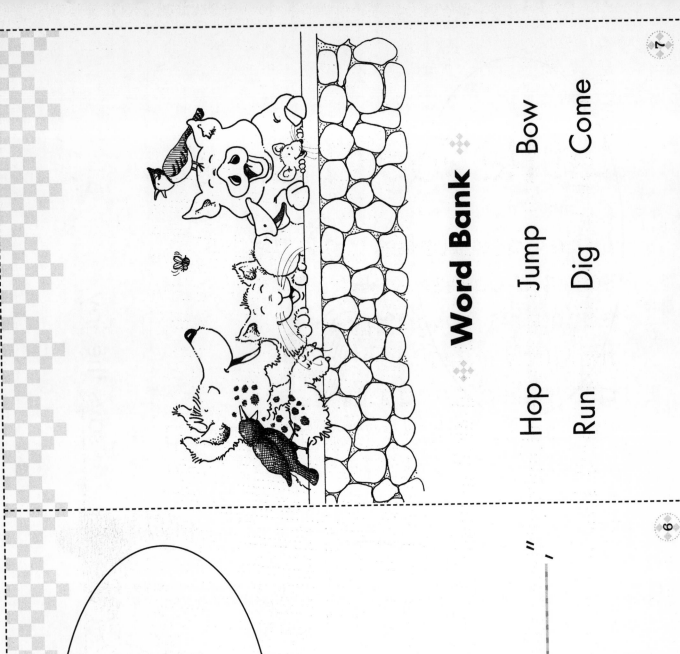

Word Bank

Hop	Jump	Bow
Run	Dig	Come

"_____"

says the rat.

7

6

Little Jack Horner

Little Jack Horner
sat in a corner
eating his holiday pie.
He stuck in his thumb
and pulled out a plum
and said, "What a lucky boy am I!"

Teaching Reading & Writing With Nursery Rhymes © 2008 by Deborah Schecter, Scholastic Teaching Resources

Phonics and Word Work
- Initial consonant blends, clusters, and digraphs
- Word building

Vocabulary
- Names for fruit

Comprehension
- Text-to-self connections

Little Jack Horner

MATERIALS

- pocket chart and sentence strips, or transparency and overhead projector
- marker

Teaching Tip

▲▲▲▲▲▲▲

- For a prop to use when sharing the rhyme, see Consonant Cluster Pie, Getting Ready, page 27. When children take turns personalizing the rhyme, invite them to pantomime pulling the fruit out of the pie with their thumb.

Getting Ready

1. Write the poem (page 25) on sentence strips and place in a pocket chart. Or copy the page onto a transparency.

2. See page 7 for suggested ways to use the poetry page with your class.

Reading the Rhyme

1. Read aloud the rhyme. Then invite children to join in as you reread it. Ask, "Have you ever had a plum pie? What kind of pie is your favorite?" On chart paper or a whiteboard, list children's responses and tally how many children prefer each kind. What pie is the class favorite?

2. On subsequent readings, let children take turns personalizing the rhyme, substituting their names and the fruit of their choice.

3. Reread the rhyme and focus on consonant blends and clusters. Point out the word *plum*, and underline or highlight the letters *pl*. Point to each letter as you say the blend. Explain to children that when these letters appear together, they make the /pl/ sound.

4. Generate with children a list of other words that begin with *pl*. (See list, below.) Children may enjoy substituting some of these words for *plum* in the poem to come up with a very silly-sounding rhyme!

5. Repeat steps 3–4, but this time focus on the word *stuck* to introduce the consonant cluster *st* and the sound it stands for, /st/.

NOTE: The term *consonant cluster* refers to the written form of two consonants that appear together in a word in which each consonant sound is heard. *Consonant blend* refers to the spoken form.

pl Words				st Words			
place	plane	play	plow	stack	stapler	stem	stop
plaid	planet	please	plug	stair	star	step	store
plain	plant	plod	plump	stamp	start	stew	storm
plan	plate	plot	plus	stand	stay	stool	stove

Consonant Cluster Pie

In this activity, children pull out and sort "plums" from a "pie" to continue working with initial blends and clusters.

Getting Ready

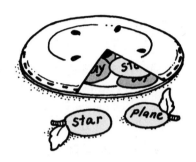

1. For each manipulative, gather a set of materials. Cut a pie-shaped "slice" out of a large paper plate. Place the plate face to face with another plate and staple them together around the edges. Color and decorate the pie. Cut steam vent slits in the top, if desired.

2. Make two copies of the plum pattern pages, and then color and cut out the plums.

3. Write words beginning with the consonant clusters *pl* and *st* on the plums. (See word lists, page 26.) Make the activity self-checking by writing the corresponding cluster on the back of each plum. Place the plums inside the pie, word side up.

4. To make sorting mats, label each small paper plate "pl" or "st."

Introducing the Activity

1. Model the activity for children. Set out the paper-plate pie that contains the *pl* and *st* plums and the two labeled paper plates.

2. Invite a volunteer to pretend to be Little Jack Horner and pull out a plum from the pie. The child reads the word on the plum and then places it on the sorting mat labeled with its beginning cluster. Repeat with the remaining plums.

3. Once children are familiar with the activity, place the materials in a center for them to use independently or in pairs. Encourage children to write on their record sheets the words they practice, organizing the words into two groups according to the beginning letters.

VARIATION: DIGRAPH PIE For practice with consonant digraphs, focus on the word *thumb* in the rhyme. Point out that sometimes two consonants at the beginning of a word make one sound. Afterward, make a digraph pie to give children more practice. On the plums, write words that begin with the consonant digraph *th*, such as *thumb*, *thank*, *three*, and *throw*. Add distracters such as *truck*, *ten*, and *take*. Have children sort and place the *th* words on a paper plate.

MATERIALS

★ plum patterns (page 29)

★ scissors

★ paper plates (two large, two small)

★ stapler

★ My Nursery Rhyme Read-and-Write Sheet (page 16)

Teaching Tip

To give the paper plate pie a just-baked smell, dot glue on the top, and then sprinkle with cinnamon. For a "sugary" topping, add glitter.

Word Endings

-ack	-ide	-ock
-ag	-ing	-ot
-ap	-ink	-ow
-aw	-ip	-ue
-ick	-ob	

l-Blend Words

bl: black, blip, blink, blob, block, blot, blow, blue

cl: clack, clap, claw, click, cling, clink, clip, clock, clot, clue

fl: flack, flag, flap, flaw, flick, fling, flip, flock, flow

gl: glide, glob glow, glue

sl: slack, slap, slaw, slick, slide, sling, slink, slip, slob, slot, slow

Phonics: Building *l*-Blend Words

Extend learning with a game that lets children build, write, and read words that begin with other *l*-blend sounds.

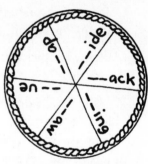

1. For each game, copy the spinner on page 30 onto sturdy paper and color. Laminate, if desired, and then cut out the pattern. Assemble the spinner using a large paper clip and brass fastener, as shown on the pattern page.

2. For each player, make a copy of the pie pattern. Write a word ending on each section, inserting lines for children to write in the missing letters. (See list at left for word endings to use and *l*-blend words that can be made.) Then cut apart the six slices.

Players: 2-3

To Play: Give each player a small paper plate and six pie slices. Review the word endings with children. Players then take turns spinning the spinner and following these directions:

1. If the spinner stops on an *l*-blend, read it and then look at your pie slices. If you can make a word using that blend and a word ending on one of the slices, write the letters on the slice. Then read aloud the word, and place the slice on your plate.

2. If the spinner stops on the plum, you may choose any *l*-blend on the spinner to try to make a word.

3. Continue playing until each player fills his or her plate with six slices.

Vocabulary: Names for Fruit

Invite children to name fruits and fillings that can be used for pies—even silly ones like watermelon! Create a word wall with their suggestions. Draw a large pie shape on craft paper and tack it to a bulletin board. To fill the pie, have children draw or cut out (from grocery ads and flyers) pictures of different fruits. Let children glue the pictures to pie-slice sections cut from paper plates and write the name for the fruit on each slice. Encourage children to use the fruit-pie word wall for ideas when they write.

Plum Patterns

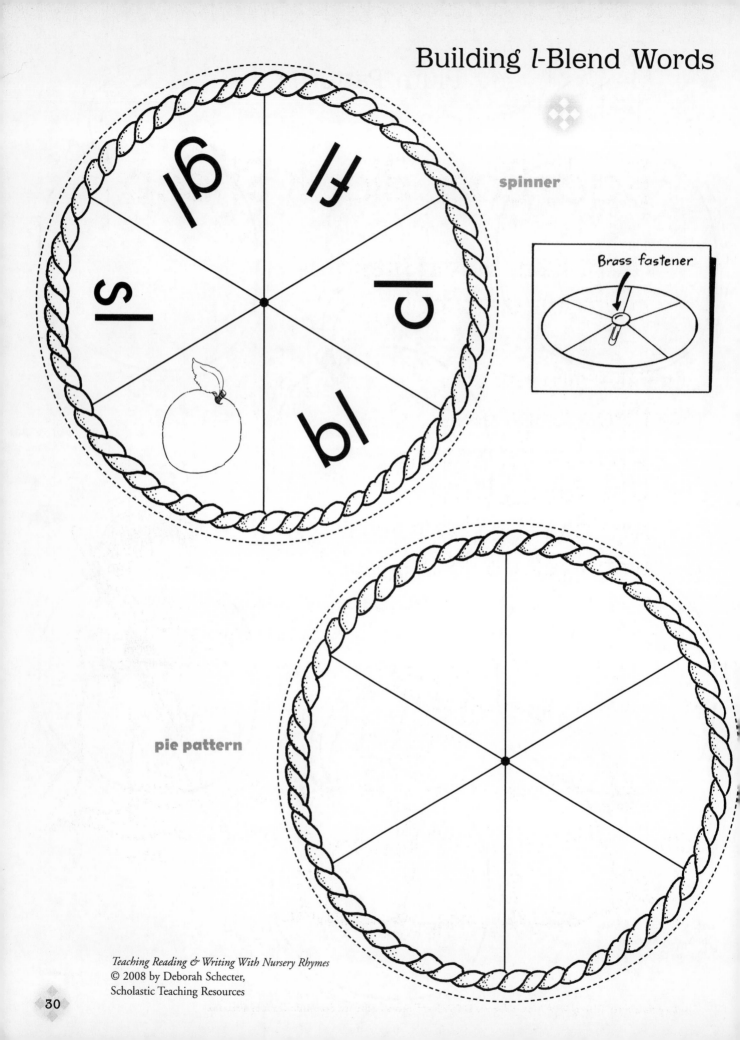

spinner

Brass fastener

pie pattern

Baa, Baa, Black Sheep

"Baa, Baa, Black Sheep
have you any wool?"

"Yes sir, yes sir,
three bags full.
One for my master.
One for my dame.
And one for the little girl
who lives down the lane."

CONCEPTS & SKILLS

Phonics
◆ Short- and long-vowel sounds

Vocabulary
◆ Color and number words

Comprehension
◆ Following a procedure

Baa, Baa, Black Sheep

MATERIALS

★ pocket chart and sentence strips, or transparency and overhead projector

★ marker

★ lambs' wool (available in pharmacies) and articles made of wool (sock, mitten, scarf, sweater)

Teaching Tip

▲▲▲▲▲▲

Bring in items made of other types of fabric such as silk, linen, cotton, and polyester for children to compare with items made of wool.

Getting Ready

1. Write the poem (page 31) on sentence strips and place in a pocket chart. Or copy the page onto a transparency.

2. See page 7 for suggested ways to use the poetry page with your class.

Reading the Rhyme

1. Before reading the rhyme, ask children to share what they know about wool. Pass around samples such as lambs' wool and a wool sock, mitten, scarf or sweater. Ask: "How does the wool feel? How are the items alike and different?"

2. Ask children if they know where wool comes from. Explain that wool comes from a sheep. (See Literature Connection, below, for related books.)

3. Tell children that you are going to share a rhyme about a sheep and its wool. Review unfamiliar words such as *master* and *dame*. Then read or sing the rhyme pointing to each word as children follow along. Invite them to chime in on a second reading. Check for understanding by asking children to retell what happens in the rhyme

4. Tell children that you're going to read the rhyme again, and this time you want them to listen for the short-*a* sound in the middle of certain words. As you read, emphasize the words—*baa, black, bag, have,* and *master.* Highlight these words and guide children to notice that although the words sound alike, they have different spelling patterns.

❖ Literature Connection ❖

Help children build background knowledge about sheep, shearing, and the process of producing wool products by sharing some of these books.

◆ *Charlie Needs a Cloak* by Tomie DePaola (Simon & Schuster, 1973). Fiction
◆ *From Sheep to Sweater* by Gail Gibbons (Holiday House, 2005). Nonfiction
◆ *Pelle's New Suit* by Elsa Beskow (Floris Books, 1989). Fiction
◆ *Wool* by Chris Oxlade (Heinemann Library, 2001). Nonfiction

Baa, Baa, Vowel Bags

Children sort a sheep's "wool" to practice distinguishing different short-vowel sounds

Getting Ready

1. Label each of five sandwich bags with one short-vowel sound: "short *a*," "short *e*," "short *i*," "short *o*," and "short *u*."

2. Write the words from the rhyme that contain short-vowel sounds (*baa, black, have, yes, bags, master, little, lives*) on self-adhesive labels or strips of masking tape. Add additional short-vowel words so that each vowel is represented a few times. Affix each word to a cotton ball and then place in the large plastic bag.

Introducing the Activity

1. Show children the bag of cotton balls and the labeled sandwich bags. Invite them to pretend that the cotton balls are pieces of wool from a sheep. Explain that they are going to help you sort the cotton balls by their vowel sounds. (Review the vowel sounds and words before proceeding.)

2. Hold up one of the cotton balls, for example, *black*, and have children read aloud the word. Have a volunteer place the cotton ball into the correct bag (in this case, short *a*). Repeat this process with each word.

3. Check that children understand what they are to do and then place the materials in a center. Invite children to visit the center, read the word on each cotton ball, and place it in the correct bag. Encourage them to record each word on their record sheet.

VARIATION: Let children explore words with long-vowel sounds by making a set of long-vowel bags. Examples in this rhyme include *sheep, three, my, dame,* and *lane.*

MATERIALS

* five plastic sandwich bags
* marker
* one-inch self-adhesive labels or masking tape
* large cotton balls
* one quart-size plastic bag
* My Nursery Rhyme Read-and-Write Sheet (page 16)

Leveling Tip

To simplify the activity, give children just one short-vowel bag, for example short *a*, and have them place in the bag only the words that contain the short-*a* sound.

Vocabulary: Color and Number Words

This rhyme can also be used to teach color and number words. Copy each line of the rhyme onto a sentence strip. Place the strips in order in a pocket chart. Then create a set of color or number word cards to replace the words *black* or *three*. Read the rhyme with children and then let them take turns choosing different color or number words to substitute and read for the ones in the rhyme.

Comprehension: Following a Procedure

Give children practice reading and following written directions to make a cute, sleepy sheep face.

1. Enlarge the project directions (page 35) and post for children to see. Or make a transparency and display on an overhead.

2. Tell children that they will be doing an art project, but first they need to read and understand the directions—the steps that explain how to make it. Discuss the importance of reading to perform a task and then read aloud the directions.

   ⭐ Point out the ordinals (*first, second, third*), and explain that these words indicate the order of the steps. Ask, "Why is it important to follow the steps in order?"

   ⭐ Guide children to notice key action words (*trace, cut, glue*) that indicate what to do in each step. What supplies do these action words suggest might be needed? (*pencils, scissors, paper,* and so on).

3. Review and model each step so that children understand what to do. Then display the directions in a center and assemble the materials needed for the activity on a tray or in a box lid. Invite children to take turns visiting the center to create sheep.

MATERIALS

⭐ *Make a Sleepy Sheep* directions (page 35)

⭐ black construction paper (cut in half the short way)

⭐ pencils

⭐ white crayons

⭐ cotton balls

⭐ glue

⭐ scissors

Make a Sleepy Sheep

First:

Lay your hand on the paper.

Keep your middle fingers together.

Trace around your hand.

Second:

Cut out the shape.

 This is your sheep's head.

Third:

Use a white crayon to **draw**

2 ● ⊥

two sleepy eyes, a nose, and a mouth.

Fourth:

Glue cotton balls

on your sheep's head.

Shhh! Don't make a peep!
Your sheep is asleep!

Teaching Reading & Writing With Nursery Rhymes © 2008 by Deborah Schecter, Scholastic Teaching Resources

Little Bo-Peep

Little Bo-Peep
has lost her sheep,
and doesn't know where to find them.
Leave them alone, and they'll come home,
wagging their tails behind them.

Little Bo-Peep

CONCEPTS & SKILLS

Phonics
◆ Long- and short-vowel word families
◆ Long-e sounds

Comprehension
◆ Following a procedure (game directions)

Writing
◆ Letters (e-mail)

Getting Ready

1. Write the poem (page 36) on sentence strips and place in a pocket chart. Or copy the page onto a transparency.

2. See page 7 for suggested ways to use the poetry page with your class.

Reading the Rhyme

1. Read aloud the rhyme and then ask: "Where do you think Bo-Peep lost her sheep? How do you think she might find them?"

2. Before rereading the poem, tell children to listen and look for words that contain the word family *-eep*. Have children identify words they notice (*Bo-Peep, sheep*). Ask: "How are the words alike? How are they different?" Invite volunteers to underline the words (or point to them if you are using a pocket chart).

3. Ask children to think of other words that contain the *-eep* word family (such as *beep, cheep, deep, keep, jeep,* and *sleep*). List these on chart paper or a whiteboard.

4. Let children take turns replacing *Bo-Peep* and *sheep* in the first two lines of the poem with other words from the *-eep* word family— for example, *Little Bo-Beep has lost her jeep and doesn't know where to find it.* Write children's new rhymes on chart paper and have volunteers underline the words that share the same word family and spelling pattern.

5. To extend the lesson, use other words in the poem to explore more long-vowel word families (for example, *know, find, behind, leave, home,* and *tail*). Look at the words one at a time, and have children suggest words that rhyme (and end with the same word family). Make a list of words for each word family.

6. Repeat step 5 for words in the poem that contain short-vowel word families (*has, and, them*).

★ game board and playing components (pages 40–43)

★ game directions and answer key (page 44)

★ scissors

★ tape

★ crayons, colored pencils or markers

★ brass fastener

★ large paper clip

★ My Nursery Rhyme Read-and-Write Sheet (page 16)

Find Bo-Peep's Sheep!

In this game, children help Little Bo-Peep find her lost sheep and practice recognizing words that contain the same long- or short- vowel word families.

Getting Ready

1. Copy the game board, word cards, game markers, and sheep cards (pages 40–43) and the game directions and answer key (page 44) onto sturdy paper.

2. Cut out the two sides of the game board along the dotted lines and tape them together. Enlist children's help in coloring the game board, sheep cards, and game markers. (Have them use different colors for the game markers to set them apart.) Then laminate all of the game components for durability.

3. Cut out all of the cards and game markers, and cut apart the directions and answer key.

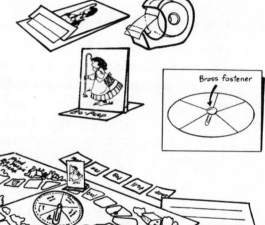

Brass fastener

4. Assemble the spinner and game markers as shown.

Introducing the Activity

1. Before children play, list on chart paper or a whiteboard all of the words from the game cards in their corresponding word family groups. Read the words aloud and then invite children to read them with you. Invite volunteers to name each picture on the game board. (NOTE: Because there are few age-appropriate long-*u* words, this game gives practice using variant-vowel phonograms for the letter *u*.)

2. Each player chooses a game marker and places it on any blank space on the game board. One player shuffles the word cards and deals five cards to each player. The remaining word cards are placed facedown in one pile and the sheep cards faceup in another pile. Then players follow the directions to play the game.

3. Review the game directions with children (order of the steps, key words). Then place the game in a center with copies of the record sheet for children to write the words they read.

Focus On . . .

Phonics: Long-*e* Sounds

Reread the rhyme and ask children to look for and listen for words that contain the long-*e* sound. Guide them to notice that *Peep* and *sheep* share the same long-*e* spelling pattern (*-ee*), while *leave* has a different one (*-ea*). With children's help, list other words that contain the long-*e* sound, grouping together words that share the same spelling pattern. (See lists, below.) Reinforce learning with this activity: Write a long-*e* word on enlarged copies of the sheep cards (page 43). While children are out of the room, hide the sheep in different spots. Later, have children search the room and find Bo-Peep's lost sheep. When they find one, have children read the word and use it in a sentence.

Long-e words

	–ea				–ee		
sea	meal	read	treat	need	deer	street	speech
eat	team	beak	dream	green	seem	freeze	three
teach	clean	real	least	feet	free	peek	tree
heat	leap	leap	speak	feel	wheel	sleep	seen

Writing: Letters (e-mail)

Give children experience composing e-mail messages by sending their own sheep-mail! Have them pretend to be Bo-Peep's sheep. Tell them to write e-mails (on copies of page 45) to inform Bo-Peep of their whereabouts. Afterward, let children practice on a real computer. (Have them send the messages to your own e-mail address and you can then reply to them as Bo-Peep!)

Teaching Tip

▲▲▲▲▲▲

Place the sheep at a center with two box lids, one labeled -ea, and the other -ee. Tell children that the lids are the sheep's pens. Have them visit the center and sort the sheep into the correct pen based on their long-*e* spelling pattern.

Find Bo-Peep's Sheep!

Baa!

Baa!

9

40

Baa!

Move ahead 2.

Move ahead 1.

Move back 1.

Move back 2.

Baa!

Baa!

Glue

deep	keep	sheep	rail	mail	tail
row	flow	know	mine	shine	fine
flag	rag	tag	due	blue	true
thing	spring	wing	tell	shell	well
junk	sunk	trunk	top	drop	shop

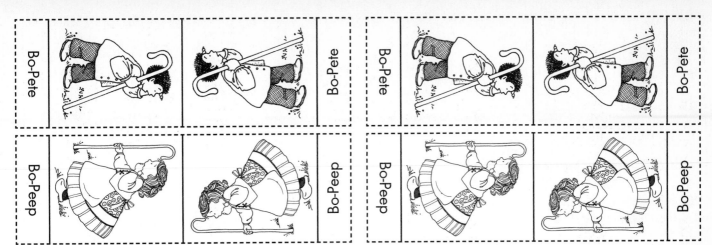

game markers

Teaching Reading & Writing With Nursery Rhymes © 2008 by Deborah Schecter, Scholastic Teaching Resources

sheep cards

43

Find Bo-Peep's Sheep!

| Players: 2 |

Game Directions

1 Spin the spinner and follow the directions. If you land on a picture, name it. Then look at your cards. Do you have a word that belongs to the same word family?

★ If you have a match, read the word and set the card aside.

★ If not, take a word card from the stack. If the new card is a match, read it, and set it aside. If the new card is not a match, your turn ends.

★ If you spin or land on a space that says, "Baa!" you may take a sheep card.

2 The first player to get rid of all of his or her cards, and find three sheep, is the winner.

3 Record the words you read on your record sheet.

Playing Rules

★ Players may land on and share the same space.

★ When no cards are left in the stack, players continue the game using the cards in their hand.

★ Players may move around the board as many times as necessary.

★ Each player may collect only three sheep in all.

Answer Key

pail: tail, mail, rail

sleep: sheep, keep, deep

nine: fine, shine, mine

bow: know, flow, row

glue: true, blue, due

bag: tag, rag, flag

bell: well, shell, tell

ring: wing, spring, thing

mop: shop drop, top

skunk: trunk, sunk, junk

Teaching Rhyming & Writing with Nursery Rhymes © 2008 by Deborah Schecter, Scholastic Teaching Resources

Sheep-mail!

Date: _____

From: _____

To: _____

Subject: _____

Message:

_____

_____

_____

_____

_____

_____

_____

The Old Woman Who Lived in a Shoe

There was an old woman
who lived in a shoe.
She had so many children,
she didn't know what to do.

She gave them some broth
along with some bread,
then hugged them all soundly
and sent them to bed.

Teaching Reading & Writing With Nursery Rhymes
© 2008 by Deborah Schecter, Scholastic Teaching Resources

The Old Woman
Who Lived in a Shoe

CONCEPTS & SKILLS

Phonics and Word Work
◆ Sight words
◆ Initial consonant blends and clusters

Writing
◆ Sentences using sight words

Vocabulary
◆ Names for homes

Comprehension
◆ Fluency
◆ Sight words in context
◆ Text-to-world connections

Getting Ready

1. Write the poem (page 46) on sentence strips and place in a pocket chart. Or copy the page onto a transparency.

2. Make multiple copies of the word card patterns (page 51). Cut them out and write a sight word from the rhyme on each one. (See list, below right.)

3. See page 7 for suggested ways to use the poetry page with your class.

Reading the Rhyme

1. Read aloud the rhyme and invite children to join in as you read it again.

2. For fun, act out the rhyme with your class. On the floor, create an outline of the Old Woman's shoe using string or yarn. Make it big enough to accommodate all of the children in your class and tape it down securely. Let one child be the Old Woman. He or she goes around to classmates, pretending to give them broth, bread, and a hug. Each child in turn then goes inside the shoe and "falls asleep."

3. On a subsequent reading, focus on the sight words in this poem. Underline or highlight each word.

4. Put the sight word cards inside the shoe or boot. Tell children to pretend that this is the home of the Old Woman and her children. Have a volunteer reach in and pull out a card and then read the sight word. Let other children offer assistance if needed. Continue this process for the remaining cards in the shoe or boot.

MATERIALS

★ pocket chart and sentence strips, or transparency and overhead projector
★ marker or highlighter
★ word card patterns (page 51)
★ string or yarn
★ tape
★ high-top shoe or boot

Sight Words in This Rhyme

This rhyme contains 22 different sight words— a few of them appearing more than once.

there	many
was	know
an	what
old	to
who	do
live[d]	gave
in	them
a	some
she	with
had	all
so	and

★ shoe house pattern
(page 52)

★ crayons, colored
pencils, or markers

★ file folder

★ glue stick

★ craft knife
(adult use only)

★ clear tape

★ sturdy white paper

★ marker

★ My Nursery Rhyme
Read-and-Write
Sheet (page 16)

Teaching Tip

▲ ▲ ▲ ▲ ▲ ▲ ▲

Use the sight word cards
(page 51) to start a word
wall. Make and display a
simple paper boot. Title
the display "So Many
Children... So Many Sight
Words!" Review with
children the sight words
from the rhyme and then
fasten the word cards to the
shoe. Beside the shoe, tack
up an envelope to hold
blank cards. Add other
sight words as children
learn them.

Sight-Word Shoe House

Children open and close the door and shutters of this shoe house to practice
reading the sight words hiding inside.

Getting Ready

1. For each manipulative, photocopy
the shoe house pattern, and then
color and cut it out. Position the
pattern on the front of a file folder
as shown, and then glue it down.

2. Cut the shoe shape out of the
folder, leaving the fold on the left
intact.

3. Open the shape and place it pattern
side up on a protected surface. Cut
through the folder to open the
shutters and door along the dotted
lines. Fold back the flaps.

4. Tape the bottom and right side of
the shoe house closed, as shown.

5. Slip a sheet of sturdy white paper
into the top of the shoe house.
Trim to fit, as needed.

6. Open the flaps and in the openings write target sight words. Create
additional word sheets by repeating this process. Place all of the word
sheets in the shoe house.

Introducing the Activity

1. Model how to use the manipulative. Open the door and shutters and
read the words inside. Then close the flaps, reopen, and invite children
to read the words aloud with you.

2. Place the manipulative in a center for children to use in pairs. Invite
them to take turns opening the flaps and reading the words inside.
Encourage children to take several turns for repeated practice of each
word, and tell them to use each word in a sentence. Have them write the
words they read on their record sheets.

3. To give children practice with a new set of words, pull out the first
sheet and place it behind the others in the shoe house.

VARIATION: Give children practice matching and reading pairs of rhyming sight words that share the same or different spelling patterns (see list, below). Make a word sheet by placing a blank sheet of paper in the shoe house and writing one of a pair of rhyming sight words in each opening. Write the corresponding rhyming word on a word card pattern (page 51). Challenge children to match the words on the cards with those in the shoe house. Encourage them to read and write the rhyming words they find.

Rhyming Sight Words

as, has	tell, well	get, let	just, must	by, buy, fly, my, try, why
at, that	take, make	drink, think	come, from	be, he, me, see, she, three, we
an, can, ran	red, said	bring, sing	day, play, say, they	light, night, right, white, write
ate, eight	clean, green	find, kind	blue, new, who, you	go, grow, know, no, show, so
keep, sleep	there, where	cold, hold	got, hot, not, stop	
walk, talk	how, now	full, pull	do, to, too, two, who	
it, sit	then, when	but, cut	all, call, fall, small, tall	

Focus On . . .

Fluency and Writing: Sentences Using Sight Words

In this activity, children practice forming, reading, and writing sentences composed of sight words.

1. Choose one of the nursery rhyme character cards (page 50) to color, cut out, and glue in the door space of a blank word sheet inside the shoe house.

2. Fill in the remaining spaces with words that children can combine to form simple sentences—for example, helping verbs such as *will*, *can*, and *may*, and verbs such as *fly*, *sing*, and *laugh*.

3. Tell children to open the door, identify the nursery rhyme character inside, and then open the shutters and read the words. Challenge them

(continues)

What the Research Says

▲ ▲ ▲ ▲ ▲ ▲

In his book *The Fluent Reader* (Scholastic, 2003), literacy specialist Timothy Rasinski points out that it is not enough for children to be able to read sight words in isolation. To help them read more fluently, provide children with opportunities to do repeated readings of sight words in the context of short phrases and sentences.

Teaching Tip

▲▲▲▲▲▲

To reinforce the spelling of each sight word, provide letter tiles (page 59) for children to spell out each word.

to form sentences using the words. For example, *Little Bo-Peep will sing* or *Little Bo-Peep can fly*. Ask children to record the sentences they make on their record sheets and then read them to a classmate.

4. As a variation, label a blank sheet inside the shoe house with sight words such as *who, what, where, when, which,* and *why*. Invite children to read each word and then use the words to write or dictate stories about favorite nursery rhyme characters.

Phonics: Initial Consonant Blends and Clusters

Use "The Old Woman Who Lived in a Shoe" to teach a mini-lesson on consonant blends and clusters. Reread the rhyme, emphasizing and underlining the letters *br* in *broth*. Tell children to search the rhyme for another word that begins with /br/ (*bread*). Then ask them to name other words that have the same beginning sound and letters as *broth* and *bread*, for example, *bring, brush,* and *brown*. List these on chart paper.

Vocabulary and Text-to-World Connections: Names for Homes

In this rhyme, a shoe is a home for the old woman and her children. Ask: "What are some real places people live?" Teach children vocabulary for different kinds of homes (*apartments, houses, houseboats, tents, hotels*). Extend the lesson to include vocabulary for different animal habitats by asking: "What's a home for a bird? A fox? A cow? A beaver?" (*nest, den, barn, lodge*). To create a "Many Kinds of Homes" word wall, make and display a large paper old-fashioned shoe shape. Invite children to draw and cut out pictures of different kinds of people and animal homes, add them to the display, and make a word label for each.

Little Boy Blue

Humpty Dumpty

Jack and Jill

Little Miss Muffet

Little Bo-Peep

nursery rhyme character cards

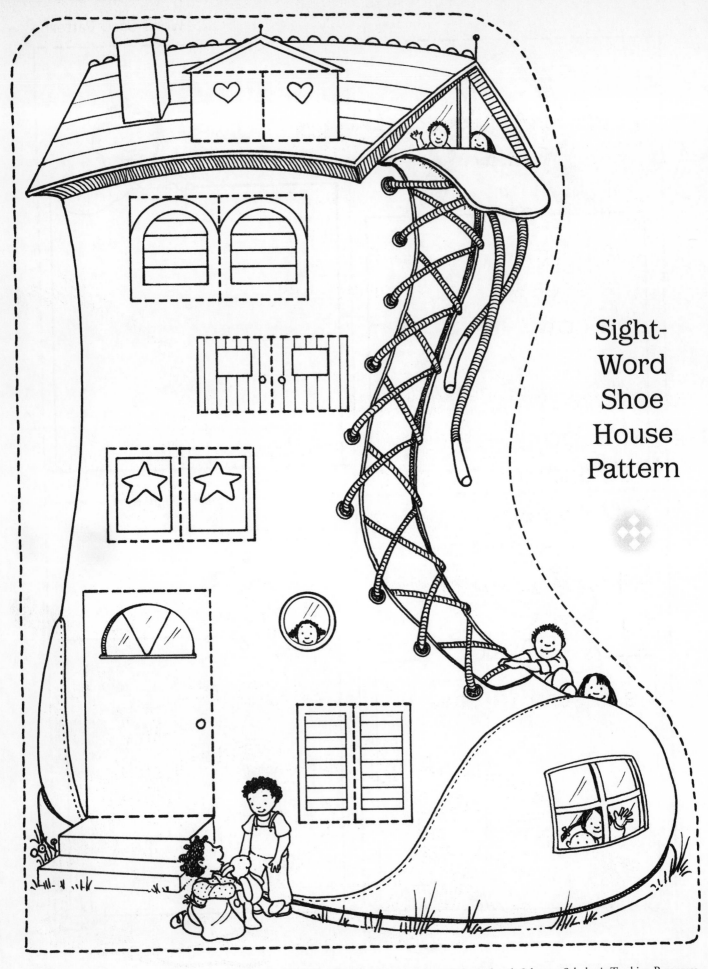

Sight-
Word
Shoe
House
Pattern

Teaching Reading & Writing With Nursery Rhymes © 2008 by Deborah Schecter, Scholastic Teaching Resources

Little Boy Blue

Little Boy Blue
come blow your horn.
The sheep's in the meadow.
The cow's in the corn.

Where is the young boy
who looks after the sheep?
He's under a haystack
fast asleep.

Will you wake him?
No, not I,
for if I do,
he is sure to cry.

Little Boy Blue

Getting Ready

1. Write the poem (page 53) on chart paper. Or copy the page onto a transparency.

2. Cut three or more sheets of yellow construction paper into haystack shapes. On each haystack, write the clues for each of three or more Word Riddles. (See examples, page 56.) Tape the tip of each haystack to the whiteboard. Then lift each haystack and use a wipe-off marker to write the riddle's answer underneath.

3. Write the chant to the right on chart paper.

4. Place the magnetic letters on the whiteboard.

5. See page 7 for suggested ways to use the poetry page with your class.

> Where, oh where
> is the word that we seek?
> It's under the haystack.
> Take a peek!

Reading the Rhyme

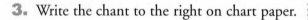

1. Begin by asking children about the jobs they do—at school and at home. Then read aloud the rhyme and ask them to explain Little Boy Blue's job. (*He tends [watches over] the farm animals and keeps them from eating crops such as corn.*) What happened? (*Little Boy Blue fell asleep. He didn't do his job, and the animals wandered into places they shouldn't have.*)

2. Reread the rhyme and then direct children's attention to the haystacks taped to the whiteboard. Tell them that a word from the poem is hidden under each one. Their job is to use the riddle clues on each haystack to figure out what the word is.

3. Read aloud the first clue and ask, "What letters do you think might be in (or not be in) this word?" Have children move magnetic letters to the side as they determine through the clues that certain letters will or will not be part of the word.

Leveling Tips

▲▲▲▲▲▲▲

To provide additional support:

◆ Mix up the magnetic letters that spell the answer and place them on the whiteboard. Add a few extras as distracters.

◆ Under each riddle, add a write-on line for each letter in the answer.

4. Read the second clue and let children narrow their guesses. (Allow children plenty of time to think.) For the last clue, invite a volunteer to come up to the board. With the other children's help, let this child manipulate letters to figure out the word.

5. Before lifting up the haystack to check the answer, invite children to recite the chant on the chart paper.

6. Repeat steps 2–5 using other haystack riddles.

Under-the-Haystack Word Riddles

MATERIALS

★ haystack word riddles (pages 57–58)

★ marker

★ letter tiles (page 59)

★ scissors

★ shoe box lid

★ whiteboard and wipe-off marker (optional)

★ My Nursery Rhyme Read-and-Write Sheet (page 16)

Children continue to analyze and build words by using clues to solve riddles.

Getting Ready

1. Copy and enlarge the haystack word riddles on sturdy paper. Write the answer to each riddle on the back. Color, laminate, and cut apart the haystacks. If desired, prepare additional haystack word riddles using copies of the blank haystack pattern. See page 56 for additional riddles.

2. Make multiple copies of the letter tiles (page 59). Laminate the pages and then cut apart the tiles.

Introducing the Activity

1. Show children one of the haystacks and read aloud the riddle. Help them work out the answer (writing possible letters and words on a whiteboard). Then recite the chant (on the chart paper) and turn over the haystack to reveal the word.

2. When children understand how to do the activity, place the haystacks, riddle side up, at a center. Provide letter tiles, a shoe box lid (to use as a letter tray), and/or a whiteboard and wipe-off marker for children to use in solving the riddles. Invite children to visit the center independently, or in pairs, to solve the riddles and write the answers on their record sheet.

3. To give children added support, do this as a whole class activity. Enlarge the haystack word riddles and tape to chart paper or a whiteboard, writing the answers under each one. Or copy onto transparencies, cut apart the haystacks, and use on an overhead.

Focus On . . .

Vocabulary: Categorizing Farm Words

This activity helps children build background knowledge and provides practice in categorizing words related to a farm. Search computer clip art, magazines, and old workbooks to find pictures of things associated with a farm (different crops, animals, buildings, machines). Glue the pictures onto index cards and label them. Randomly hand out the cards and ask children to organize themselves into different groups according to the pictures they are holding. Encourage children to confer as they form their groups. Afterward, review each group's pictures and words. Ask children to explain the reasons they grouped themselves together.

Phonics: Long Vowel Sounds

Use "Little Boy Blue" to focus on words that contain long-vowel sounds: *wake, sheep, I, blow,* and variant *u* in *blue.* Show children how to curl their hands to make Little Boy Blue's horn and practice tooting. As you read aloud the rhyme, tell children to toot two times whenever they hear a word containing a long-vowel sound.

Word Riddles

1. I have one letter.
2. I rhyme with *bye*.
3. I sound the same as *eye*.
(answer: *I*)

1. I have two letters.
2. I rhyme with *row*.
3. I am the opposite of *yes*.
(answer: *no*)

1. I have two letters.
2. You can find me inside the word *begin*.
3. The cow is __ __ the corn.
(answer: *in*)

1. I have two letters.
2. I start with the same beginning sound as *hill*.
3. I am the opposite of *she*.
(answer: *he*)

1. I have three letters.
2. I begin with the letter after *m*.
3. I end with the beginning sound of *tea*.
(answer: *not*)

1. I have the same middle sound as *boil*.
2. I end with the letter before *z*.
3. I am the opposite of *girl*.
(answer: *boy*)

1. I end with the same beginning sound as *no*.
2. Inside me, you can find the word *or*.
3. I like to eat __ __ __ __ on the cob.
(answer: *corn*)

1. I have four letters.
2. I begin with the same beginning sound as *blue*.
3. I rhyme with *show*.
(answer: *blow*)

1. I have three letters.

2. I begin with the letter before *z*.

3. I rhyme with *new*.

★ What word am I? ★

1. I end with *y*.

2. The word *to* is part of me.

3. You can play with me.

★ What word am I? ★

1. I have fewer than three letters.

2. I start with the same beginning sound as *dot*.

3. I rhyme with *who*.

★ What word am I? ★

1. I start with *h*.

2. I have the same middle sound as *fork*.

3. I go, "toot-toot-toot!"

★ What word am I? ★

1. I have four letters.

2. I start with the same beginning sound as *blow*.

3. I am a color.

★ What word am I? ★

Answers, clockwise from top left: *you, toy, horn, blue, do.*

1. I start with the same ending sound as *tub*.
2. You can read me.
3. I rhyme with *cook*.

★ What word am I? ★

1. I have three letters.
2. I have the same middle sound as *house*.
3. I say "moo!"

★ What word am I? ★

1. I have fewer than four letters.
2. I begin with the same ending sound as *how*.
3. I am the opposite of *in*.

★ What word am I? ★

1. I am a number.
2. I end with the same ending sound as *roar*.
3. 5 – 1 = *me*!

★ What word am I? ★

1. I end with double consonants.
2. I begin with the letter after *g*.
3. I rhyme with *will*.

★ What word am I? ★

1. I begin with the same beginning sound as *cry*.
2. I rhyme with *frown*.
3. A king wears a _ _ _ _ _.

★ What word am I? ★

Answers, clockwise from top left: *book, cow, four, crown, hill, out.*

Letter Tiles

a	b	c	d	e	f	g	h	i	j
k	l	m	n	o	p	q	r	s	t
u	v	w	x	y	z	a	b	c	d
e	f	g	h	i	j	k	l	m	n
o	p	q	r	s	t	u	v	w	x
y	z	a	b	c	d	e	f	g	h
i	j	k	l	m	n	o	p	q	r
s	t	u	v	w	x	y	z	a	e
i	o	u	a	e	i	o	u	a	e
i	o	u	a	e	i	o	u	a	e
i	o	u	a	e	i	o	u	a	e
i	o	u	a	e	i	o	u	a	e

hing Reading & Writing With Nursery Rhymes © 2008 by Deborah Schecter, Scholastic Teaching Resources

59

The Itsy Bitsy Spider

The itsy bitsy spider
climbed up the waterspout.
Down came the rain
and washed the spider out.
Out came the sun
and dried up all the rain.
And the itsy bitsy spider
climbed up the spout again.

The Itsy Bitsy Spider

Getting Ready

1. Write the poem (page 60) on sentence strips and place in a pocket chart. Or copy the page onto a transparency.

2. See page 7 for suggested ways to use the poetry page with your class.

Reading the Rhyme

1. Before sharing the rhyme, discuss what children know about spiders Ask: "Have you ever seen a spider? Where? What did you notice about the spider?"

2. Read or sing the rhyme aloud and then ask children if they know what a waterspout is. If possible, take children outdoors to show them a waterspout attached to a building. Explain that the spout carries rainwater away from the building.

3. Take a closer look at the word *waterspout*. Write the word on chart paper or a whiteboard and ask children what they notice about it. Guide them to recognize that it is made up of two words: *water* and *spout*. Invite children to explain how looking at the two word parts helps them understand the meaning of the whole word. Brainstorm other compound words that begin with *water* (*waterfall, waterproof, watermelon, watercolors*) and discuss their meaning. For more word-building investigations, see Word-Ladder Waterspout (page 62).

4. Discuss with children the repeating circular story pattern in this rhyme. The rhyme begins and ends with the spider climbing up the spout.

MATERIALS

- ★ pocket chart and sentence strips, or transparency and overhead projector
- ★ marker

Nonfiction Connection

Make a KWL chart to record what children know about spiders and what they would like to find out. Then share some of these nonfiction books about spiders to research answers to their questions.

- *Spiders* by Nik Bishop (Scholastic, 2007).
- *Spiders* by Gail Gibbons (Holiday House, 1993).
- *Spiders Are Not Insects* by Allan Fowler (Children's Press, 1996).
- *Spinning Spiders* by Ruth Berman (Lerner, 1998).

- word-ladder waterspouts (pages 65–66)
- spider patterns page 63
- scissors
- wipe-off markers
- 12-inch piece of yarn
- tape
- resealable sandwich bags
- My Nursery Rhyme Read-and-Write Sheet (page 16)

Teaching Tip

▲▲▲▲▲▲▲

Copy the word-ladder spout, spider pattern, and letter tiles onto transparencies and use on an overhead projector to model the activity for children.

❖ Word-Ladder Waterspout ❖

Children deconstruct words to form new ones and help the spider climb the waterspout.

Getting Ready

1. Copy one spider pattern (page 63) and page 65. Color as desired, laminate, and cut out.

2. Cut off the letter tile strip at the bottom of page 65 and cut apart the letters.

3. Punch a hole through the circles on the spout and spider. Thread the yarn through the spider, poke each end of the yarn through a hole on the spout, and tape to the back. Check that the spider slides easily along the yarn.

4. Use the blank spout template, suggested sets of words, and picture strips (pages 66–67) to make additional word ladder activities. (Mask or add extra letter boxes as needed.)

5. Make multiple copies of the letter tiles (page 59). Laminate and cut apart the letters. Store the tiles in a resealable bag.

Introducing the Activity

1. Read aloud the directions and show children the seven letter tiles they will use. Also show them how to slide the spider up and down the spout.

2. Point to the picture directly above "Start here." Say the name of the picture, *rain*, and then build the word by placing one letter tile in each box. Invite children to read the completed word aloud. Then demonstrate how to write the letters in the boxes to replace the letter tiles.

3. Now that the first word is complete, invite a volunteer to slide the spider up so it is beside the word *rain*.

4. Go to the next picture. Name the picture, *run*, and then ask children how this word sounds different from *rain*. (*The middle sound is different.*) Work with children to build the new word. Have them compare the spelling to the first word to find letters that were changed, added, or deleted.

5. Repeat this process with each new word until you complete the word in the top row, *sun*, and the spider has climbed to the top of the spout. Point out to children that they have turned *rain* into *sun*! (The words on the completed ladder, from bottom to top, should be: *rain, run, fan, fun, sun*.)

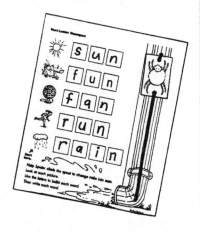

6. Read the list of words aloud, moving from bottom to top. Invite children to read aloud with you. Then place the manipulative in a center for children to use independently or in pairs. Encourage them to write the words they build on their record sheet.

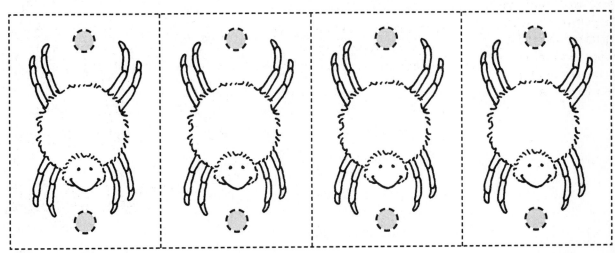

spider patterns

Phonics: Diphthongs

Highlight the words in the rhyme that contain the diphthong /ou/ (*spout, out, down*) Ask children how these words are alike. (*They all contain the /ou/ sound.*) Point out that these words share the same sound but this sound can be spelled in different ways. Encourage children to name other words that have the /ou/ sound. List these on chart paper. Then challenge children to come up with variations of the "The Itsy Bitsy Spider" using words from the list. For example:

> The itsy bitsy spider went into town.
> On the way there, she met a funny clown.
>
> The itsy bitsy spider crawled along the ground.
> A tasty bug for lunch is what she found!

Comprehension: Retelling and Sequencing

Have children use the spout pattern and spider to practice retelling and sequencing.

1. Make copies of the spider pattern (page 63) and just the spout illustration from page 66.

2. Draw four horizontal lines to the left of the illustration and a line at the top for a title. Then attach the spider to the spout. (See page 62, step 3.)

3. Starting from the bottom and working their way to the top of the spout, ask children to write or draw a picture that describes each key event in the poem. Encourage them to use words such as *first, next, then,* and *last* to show sequence.

4. Invite children to slide the spider up the spout as they retell the poem to a classmate. Encourage them to take their story spouts home to share with family members as well.

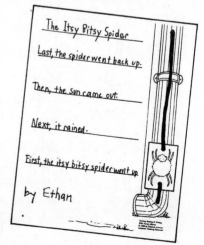

My Word-Ladder Waterspout: _____

	f	u	n

Start here.

Help Spider climb the spout to change **rain** into **sun**.

Look at each picture.

Use the letters to build each word.

Then write each word.

Teaching Reading & Writing With Nursery Rhymes © 2008 by Deborah Schecter, Scholastic Teaching Resources

f r i n u a s

My Word-Ladder Waterspout: _____

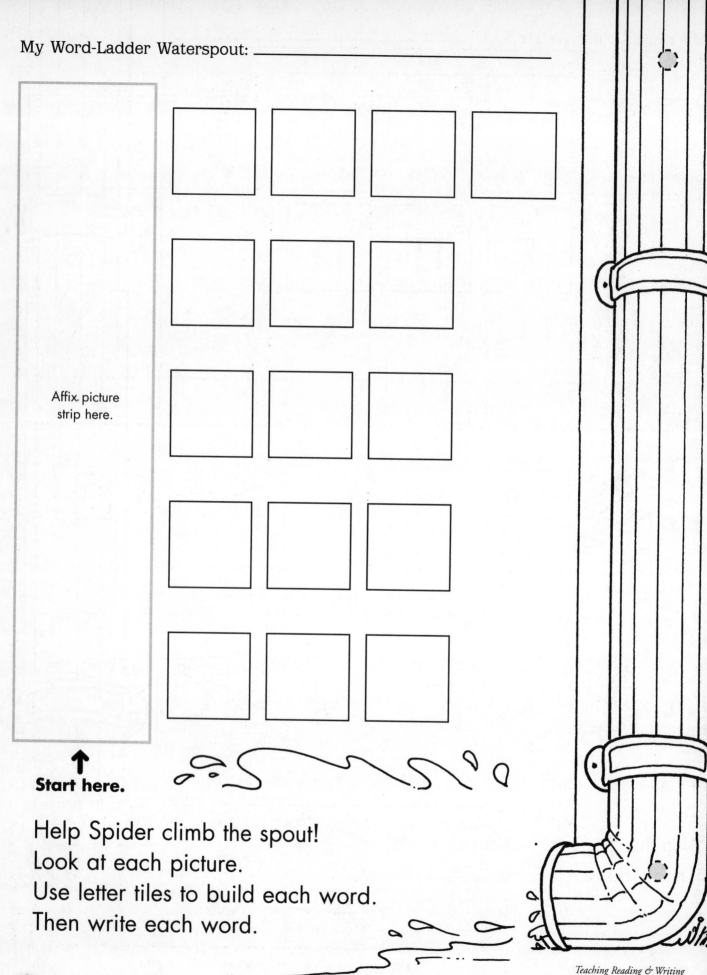

Affix picture
strip here.

↑
Start here.

Help Spider climb the spout!
Look at each picture.
Use letter tiles to build each word.
Then write each word.

*Teaching Reading & Writing
With Nursery Rhymes*
© 2008 by Deborah Schecter,
Scholastic Teaching Resources

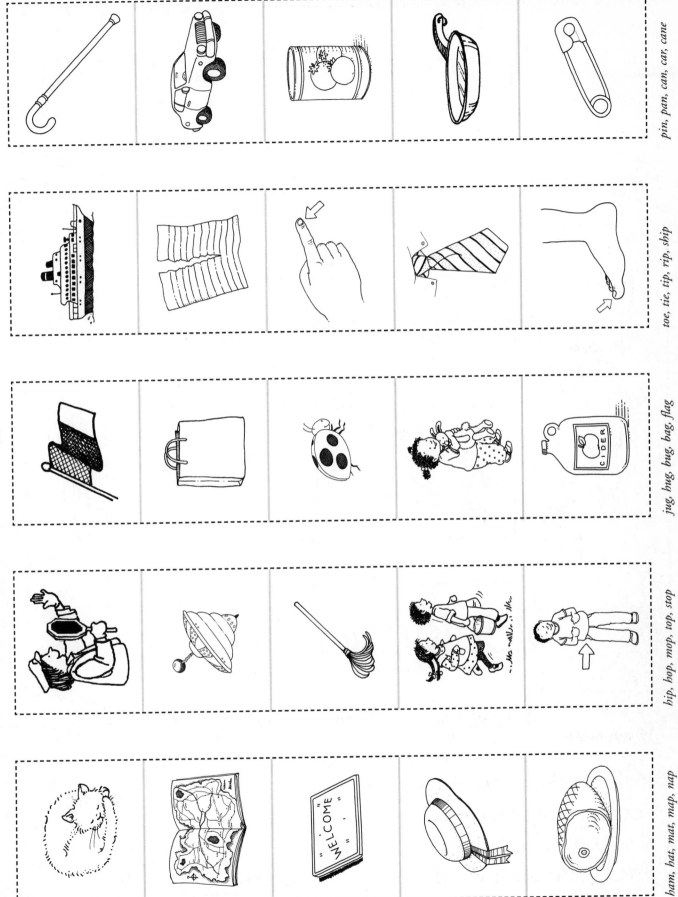

pin, pan, can, car, cane

toe, tie, tip, rip, ship

jug, hug, bug, bag, flag

hip, hop, mop, top, stop

ham, hat, mat, map, nap

Jack and Jill

Jack and Jill went up the hill
to fetch a pail of water.
Jack fell down and broke his crown,
and Jill came tumbling after.

Teaching Reading & Writing With Nursery Rhymes © 2008 by Deborah Schecter, Scholastic Teaching Resources

Jack and Jill

CONCEPTS & SKILLS

Vocabulary
◆ Synonyms
◆ Action words
◆ Positional words and phrases

Writing
◆ Word Bank Books

Comprehension
◆ Using context clues
◆ Text-to-self connections

Getting Ready

1. Write the poem (page 68) on sentence strips and place in a pocket chart. Or copy the page onto a transparency.

2. See page 7 for suggested ways to use the poetry page with your class.

Reading the Rhyme

1. Read aloud the rhyme and discuss unfamiliar vocabulary:

   ★ Ask children what they think the word *fetch* means. You may want to write the word on chart paper and help children make a web with synonyms. Why do Jack and Jill need to fetch water? (*Sometimes people get their water from a well and they carry it home in buckets.*)

   ★ How about the word *crown*? Is Jack wearing a crown? Guide children to understand that *crown* refers to Jack's head.

2. Read the rhyme again. To help children make text-to-self connections, ask them to tell about times they have fallen while playing tag or another game. Ask: "Were you hurt? What happened afterward? How might Jack have gotten better?"

3. Ask children to read along as you reread the rhyme. Point to the word *went* and explain that it is an action word that describes movement.

4. Use a self-sticking note to cover *went* in the rhyme. Ask children to think of a different action word to describe how Jack and Jill might get up the hill, for example, *run, hop,* or *skip.* (For simplicity, use words in the present tense.) Write the word on the sticky note and together read the revised rhyme. Invite two volunteers to act it out.

5. With children, generate a list of other action words (serious or silly!) to use in the rhyme. (See list, page 70.) Write the words on chart paper or a whiteboard. Then repeat step 4, substituting action words, reading the new versions, and letting children act them out.

MATERIALS

★ pocket chart and sentence strips, or transparency and overhead projector

★ marker

★ self-sticking notes

gather

pick up   collect

fetch

bring back   get

go for

* wheel patterns (pages 72–73)
* scissors
* crayons
* thin-tipped markers or colored pencils
* brass fastener
* My Nursery Rhyme Read-and-Write Sheet (page 16)

Jack and Jill Action-Word Wheel

Children turn this wheel to practice reading and writing action words.

Getting Ready

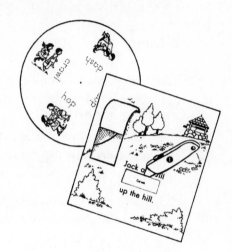

1. For each manipulative, photocopy the wheel patterns onto sturdy paper and cut them out.

2. On the hill scene (the top pattern), cut out the word window and cut open the flap along the dotted lines. Poke a hole through the center dot in each pattern as indicated.

Introducing the Activity

1. Give each child the two parts of the manipulative and markers or colored pencils. Invite children to color the pictures as desired.

2. Give each child a brass fastener. Show children how to join the two parts of the manipulative using the fastener. To use, children hold the manipulative in one hand and use their other hand to turn the bottom wheel until the word *hop* appears in the window. (The flap should be closed.) Together, read the sentence.

3. Invite children to lift the flap to see the picture. Encourage them to talk about how the illustration corresponds to the word *hop*.

4. Tell children to use a marker or colored pencil to trace each letter of the word. Then invite them to take turns reading the completed sentence.

5. Continue in this manner with the remaining words until children have read and traced all four words. Have children write each complete sentence on the record sheet.

Action Words for Movement

bike	hurry	ride	scurry	spring	tumble
bolt	jog	roll	skate	sprint	twirl
creep	leap	rush	skip	stomp	wiggle
fly	march	scamper	slide	stroll	zip
hike	race	scoot	spin	tiptoe	zoom

❖ Focus On . . . ❖

Teaching Tip

▲▲▲▲▲▲

Have children make word-bank books for other categories such as describing words, opposites, or synonyms.

Writing: Word Banks

Let children make word-bank books to record words they are learning and to use as a reference in their writing.

1. Ahead of time, make a class set of the large well pattern (page 74). Then review with children the list of action words made earlier.

2. Give each child a well pattern and several sheets of lined paper. Show children how to place the well on top of the sheets of paper and staple on the left side. Then instruct them to cut out the well along the dotted lines, cutting through the lined paper as they do so. Let children decorate, as desired.

3. On the cover, have children fill in the word *Action* and their name. Tell them to write and illustrate different action words inside. They can add to their booklets as they encounter new words in their reading.

■ M A T E R I A L S ■

⭐ small well, Jack, and Jill patterns (page 74)
⭐ scissors
⭐ brown paper lunch bag
⭐ small rock (or other heavy object)
⭐ stapler
⭐ index cards
⭐ plastic pail
⭐ crayons, colored pencils, or markers
⭐ craft sticks
⭐ tape

Vocabulary: Positional Words

Jack and Jill go *up* and then *down* the hill. Use this rhyme to give children practice using other positional words and phrases.

1. Use scissors to round the top of a paper lunch bag so it resembles a hill. Place a rock or other heavy object in the bag for stability.

2. Copy, color, and cut out the small well pattern (page 74). Staple the well to the top of the bag, stapling the bag closed as you do so.

3. On index cards, write short sentences using various positional words and phrases, such as *Jill is in front of Jack*, or *Jack is beside the well*. Place these in a plastic pail (or another container.)

4. Have children make Jack and Jill puppets. Copy the patterns (page 74) onto sturdy paper. Have children color, cut them out, and tape to craft sticks.

5. Let children take turns selecting cards from the pail and using the puppets and the well on the hill to act out the sentences.

Jack and Jill
Action-Word Wheel

Jack and Jill

Cut out.

up the hill.

Teaching Reading & Writing With Nursery Rhymes © 2008 by Deborah Schecter, Scholastic Teaching Resources

Jack and Jill
Action-Word Wheel

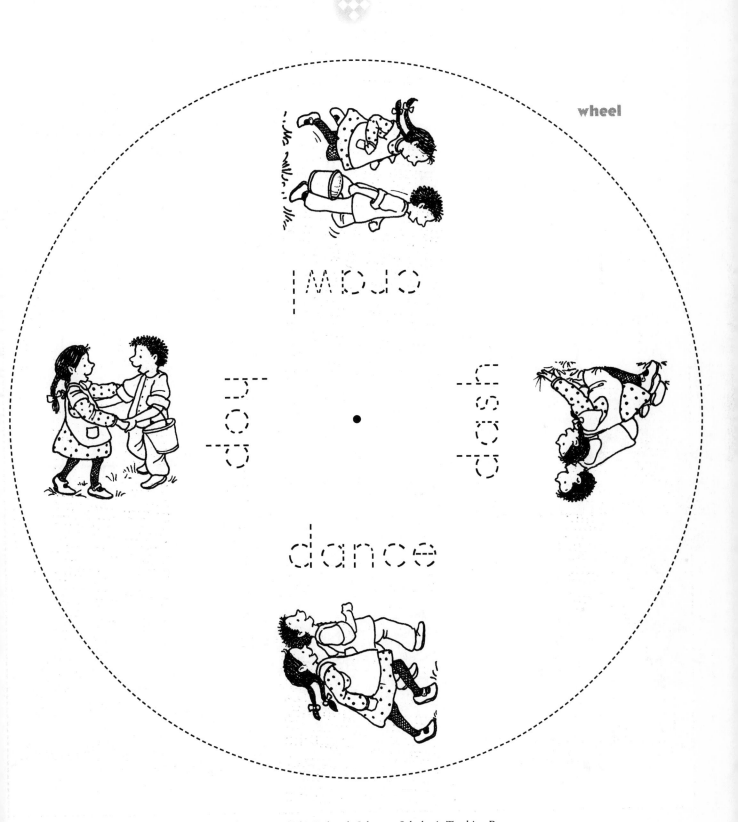

wheel

crawl

pour

open

dance

Jack puppet

Jill puppet

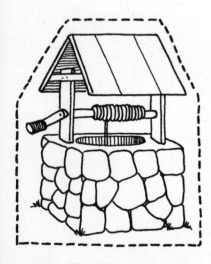

small well pattern

Well Book
Pattern

My Well

of _____

Words

By _____

Teaching Reading & Writing With Nursery Rhymes © 2008 by Deborah Schecter, Scholastic Teaching Resources

Hey, Diddle, Diddle

Hey, Diddle, Diddle,
the cat and the fiddle.
The cow jumped over the moon.
The little dog laughed to see such fun.
And the dish ran away with the spoon.

CONCEPTS & SKILLS

Comprehension
◆ Real versus fantasy

Vocabulary and Writing
◆ Positional words and phrases

Phonics and Word Work
◆ Words with double letters

Hey, Diddle, Diddle

MATERIALS

★ pocket chart and sentence strips
★ marker
★ cow and moon patterns (page 79)
★ scissors
★ crayons, colored pencils, or markers
★ large craft sticks
★ tape

Teaching Tip

▲▲▲▲▲▲

To reinforce and assess learning, invite children to copy (or dictate) on a sheet of paper the third line of the rhyme, leaving a blank for the word *over*. Ask them to complete the sentence with the word of their choice and then illustrate their sentences.

Getting Ready

1. Write the poem (page 75) on sentence strips and place in a pocket chart. Photocopy the cow and moon patterns (page 79) onto cardstock. Color and cut out the patterns and tape each to a craft stick.

2. Write various positional words and phrases on sentence strips and trim to size. Examples: *over, under, next to, off, on, in front of, in back of, around.* Place these in the pocket chart.

3. See page 7 for suggested ways to use the poetry page with your class.

Reading the Rhyme

1. Read aloud the rhyme. Then ask: "Could a cow really jump over the moon? Could a dish run away with a spoon?" Invite children to comment on the funny, make-believe events in the rhyme.

2. Read the rhyme again, using the cow and moon stick puppets to act out the third line, "The cow jumped over the moon." Then invite children to take turns using the puppets to act out the same line as the rest of the class rereads it.

3. Give children practice using other positional words and phrases. Review with them the positional word and phrase cards. Then cover the word *over* with one of the word or phrase cards. Read the revised sentence together.

4. Invite a volunteer to use the puppets to show the cow doing the action described. Continue this process using the other cards and letting other children take turns.

Positional Word Pull-Through

The antics of the zany cow in this rhyme will help children practice using positional words.

Getting Ready

1. Photocopy pages 80–81 onto sturdy paper and then color and cut out the pieces. Laminate, if desired.

2. Cut along the four dotted lines on the cow.

3. Weave the word strip through the first pair of slits on the left side of the cow. Repeat with the picture strip on the right side.

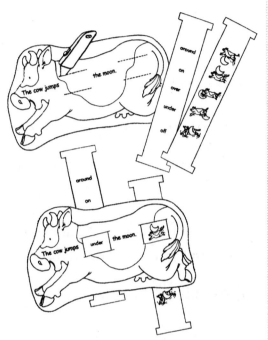

Introducing the Activity

1. Model for children how to gently pull the picture strip to reveal a picture—for example, the picture of the cow jumping over the moon. Ask, "What sentence describes what is happening in this picture?"

2. Pull the word strip until the word *over* appears. Read the sentence aloud. Then ask children to read it with you.

3. Repeat this process a few times, matching picture and word strips.

4. Choose another picture—for example, the picture of the cow jumping under the moon. But this time pull the word strip to create a sentence that does not describe it, such as *The cow jumps off the moon.* Read the sentence aloud with children and discuss why the picture and sentence are not a match.

5. Check that children understand how to pull the strips to reveal a picture and then form and read the sentence that describes it. Then place the manipulatives in a center. When children visit the center, have them write the sentences they make on the record sheet.

MATERIALS

★ cow pattern (page 80)

★ word and picture strips (page 81)

★ scissors

★ crayons, colored pencils, or markers

★ craft knife (adult use only)

★ My Nursery Rhyme Read-and-Write Sheet (page 16)

Teaching Tips

◆ For an added challenge, leave off the picture strip. Ask children to form, read, and write sentences.

◆ To make the activity self-checking, write a number directly behind each word on the word strip. Write the same number behind the corresponding picture on the picture strip.

Writing: Positional Words

Use other lines in "Hey, Diddle, Diddle" to give children more practice with positional words and phrases. For example, write the following sentence frame on chart paper or a whiteboard: *The dish ran away _____ the spoon.* Brainstorm with children words they might use to complete the sentence, such as *before, after, beside, from, to the left of, to the right of,* and *behind.* For added fun and to assess comprehension, let children act out the revised lines using a plastic dish and large spoon as props.

Phonics: Words With Double Letters

Revisit the rhyme and ask children if they can spot words that contain double letters (*diddle, fiddle, moon, spoon, little, see*). Invite children to be on the lookout for words with double letters in other nursery rhymes they read, for example, "Baa, Baa, Black Sheep" (page 31), "Jack and Jill" (page 68), "Humpty Dumpty" (page110), and "Three Little Kittens" (page 131).

Cow and Moon
Puppet Patterns

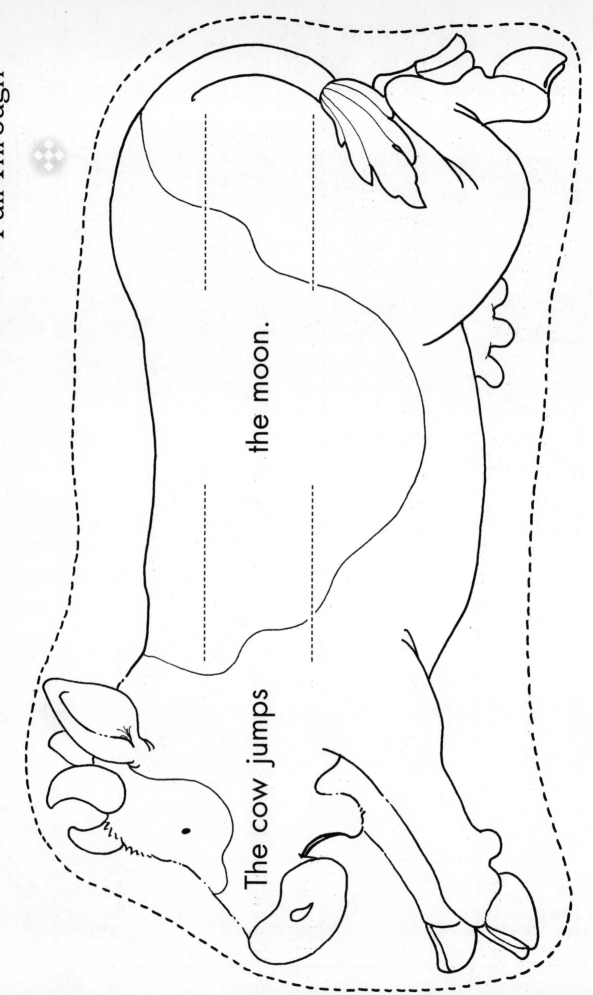

the moon.

The cow jumps

Teaching Reading & Writing With Nursery Rhymes
© 2008 by Deborah Schecter, Scholastic Teaching Resources

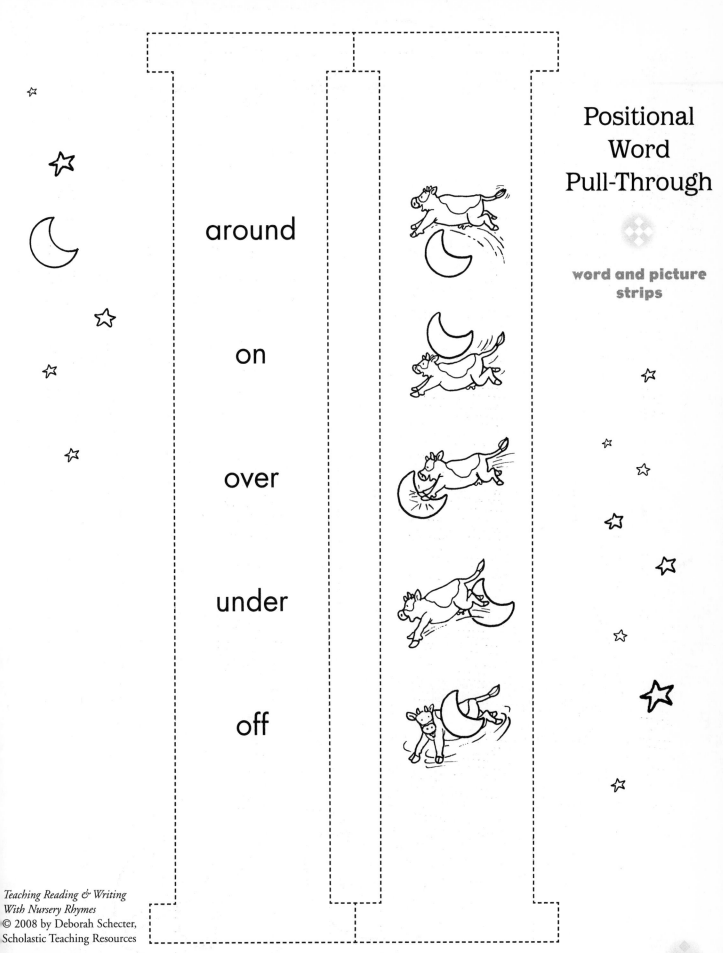

Positional Word Pull-Through

word and picture strips

around

on

over

under

The Queen of Hearts

The Queen of Hearts,
she made some tarts,
all on a summer's day.
The Knave of Hearts,
he stole the tarts,
and with them ran away.

The King of Hearts
called for the tarts,
and scolded the Knave full score.
The Knave of Hearts
brought back the tarts,
and vowed he'd steal no more.

The Queen of Hearts

CONCEPTS & SKILLS

Vocabulary and Writing
- Shape words
- Descriptive language
- Bakery words

Comprehension
- Following a procedure (game directions)
- Predicting outcomes
- Making inferences

Getting Ready

1. Write the poem (page 82) on chart paper. Or copy it onto a transparency.

2. For the activity in Reading the Rhyme, step 5 (page 84), write each of the first six lines of the poem on sentence strips. Cut the second and fifth lines into two parts as shown. Place the strips in a pocket chart.

The Queen of Hearts,
she made some	tarts,
all on a summer's day.
The Knave of Hearts,
he stole the	tarts,
and with them ran away.

Circle	diamond	oval
heart	square	half circle
rectangle	triangle

3. Write shape words (see Materials, right) on additional sentence strips (make two for each shape word), trim to size, and place at the bottom of the pocket chart.

4. See page 7 for suggested ways to use the poetry page with your class.

Reading the Rhyme

1. Read aloud the rhyme. Then discuss words and phrases that may be unfamiliar to children, such as *tart* (a pastry similar to a small pie, often filled with jam, fruit, or custard), *knave* (someone who is a servant; someone who is tricky or dishonest), *full score* (20 times), and *vowed* (promised). Then show children the Queen, King, and Jack playing cards. Explain that this rhyme brings these playing card characters to life and that *Jack* is another word for *knave*.

2. Discuss what happens in the rhyme. Ask children what they think of the knave's behavior. Why did he return the tarts? Did he learn a lesson? Discuss honesty. Why is it important to be honest? If the knave had wanted some tarts, what might he have done instead of stealing them?

(continues)

MATERIALS

- chart paper or transparency and overhead projector
- sentence strips and pocket chart
- marker
- Queen, King, and Jack playing cards (heart suits)
- construction paper shapes (diamonds, squares, rectangles, triangles, hearts, ovals, circles, half circles)
- plastic tray
- paper lunch bag

Teaching Tip

▲▲▲▲▲▲▲▲

For an activity that lets children practice predicting outcomes, see Focus On . . . Comprehension (page 85). Try this before sharing the second verse of this rhyme.

Use children's performance of the rhyme as an opportunity to introduce descriptive vocabulary. For example:

◆ Give the queen a tray and the paper tarts. She can pantomime *mixing* the ingredients, *rolling* the dough, *forming* the tarts, *baking* them in the oven, and *arranging* the *freshly-baked* tarts on the tray.

◆ Give the knave a paper bag. The knave can smell the *delicious aroma* of the tarts, *tiptoe* up to the queen, *snatch* the tarts, *stash* them in the bag, and *sneak* away.

◆ Upon discovering that his tarts have been stolen, the king can look *furious* and *furrow his brow* as he *stomps* around and then *scolds* the knave.

MATERIALS

★ game board (page 86)

★ game directions and tart cards (page 87)

★ crayons, colored pencils, or markers

★ scissors

★ tape

★ two paper plates

3. Once children are familiar with the rhyme, let groups of three take turns acting it out. (Children can make and decorate tagboard crowns for the king and queen to wear.) See Teaching Tip, left, for more.

4. Point to the hearts on the Queen of Hearts playing card. Have children find the word *hearts* in the rhyme. Then find out what other shapes children know. Hold up each paper shape in turn and ask children to name it. Invite volunteers to point to the word card for each shape in the pocket chart.

5. On subsequent readings, use the pocket chart to innovate on the text. Insert a shape word in front of the word *tarts* in the second and fifth lines. Invite children to read the revised version with you. For example, these lines might read, *She made some triangle tarts* and *He stole the triangle tarts.* When children act out the rhyme, the knave should take only the triangle-shaped tarts. Let children take turns playing the role of knave so that each child gets practice with a shape word.

❖ Rescue the Tarts! Game ❖

In this game, children identify different shapes to refill the Queen of Hearts' plate with tarts.

Getting Ready

1. For each game, make two copies each of the game board and tart cards. Make one copy of the game directions.

2. Enlist children's help in coloring the game boards and tart patterns. Laminate the game parts, if desired, and cut them out.

Introducing the Activity

1. Show children the tart cards and a game board. Hold up one card at a time and ask children to name its shape. Invite a volunteer to find the word for that shape on the game board and cover it with the tart card.

2. Divide the class into pairs and give each pair two game boards, two sets of cards, and the game directions. (Or place the game in a center for pairs of children to use independently.) Review the directions (order of the steps, key words). Each player then takes a game board plate. One player mixes up the cards and places them facedown near the game boards. Players then take turns following the game directions.

Writing: Shape Words

In this mini-book, children practice reading and writing the words for different shapes.

1. Copy pages 88–89 for each child (enlarge if desired), and have children cut apart the pages. Read the text on each page with children.

2. Explain that children are going to help the Queen of Hearts make her tarts. To do this, they will read the shape word on each page, trace the letters, and then draw and decorate a tart in that shape. (Provide glitter glue, sequins, and other craft materials for children to use, if desired.) Assess children's understanding of the words by observing them as they work.

3. Ask children what they should do on the last page. (*Write the numeral 6 on the blank line and draw pictures of all of the tarts.*)

4. To assemble their mini-books, have children stack pages 1–6 in order and then staple them to the right side of page 7, along the top. Have children write their name on the back of the book.

5. Together, read the completed book. Then invite children to take turns reading their mini-books to a classmate.

Comprehension: Predicting Outcomes

When reading the rhyme for the first time with children, stop after the first verse and ask, "What do you think might happen next? Why?" Give each child a sheet of paper. Direct children to fold the paper in half. On the outside of the folded paper, invite children to draw or write about what they think might happen next in the rhyme. Encourage children to share their ideas with classmates. After reading the rest of the poem, have them open the paper and use words and pictures to tell what really did happen. Ask: "How did your prediction compare with what really happened in the rhyme? Which ending do you prefer? Why?"

Vocabulary: Bakery Words

Beside tarts, what other bakery treats might the Queen of Hearts make? Invite children to search grocery ads and flyers for examples, such as *cupcakes, cookies, pies, cakes, doughnuts, brownies, muffins,* and *turnovers.* Create a word wall of bakery items by drawing the outline of a bakery showcase on craft paper and adding lines for shelves. Tack up pictures children find (or draw), adding a word label to each. Invite children to refer to the word wall whenever they want to add a tasty bakery treat to their writing.

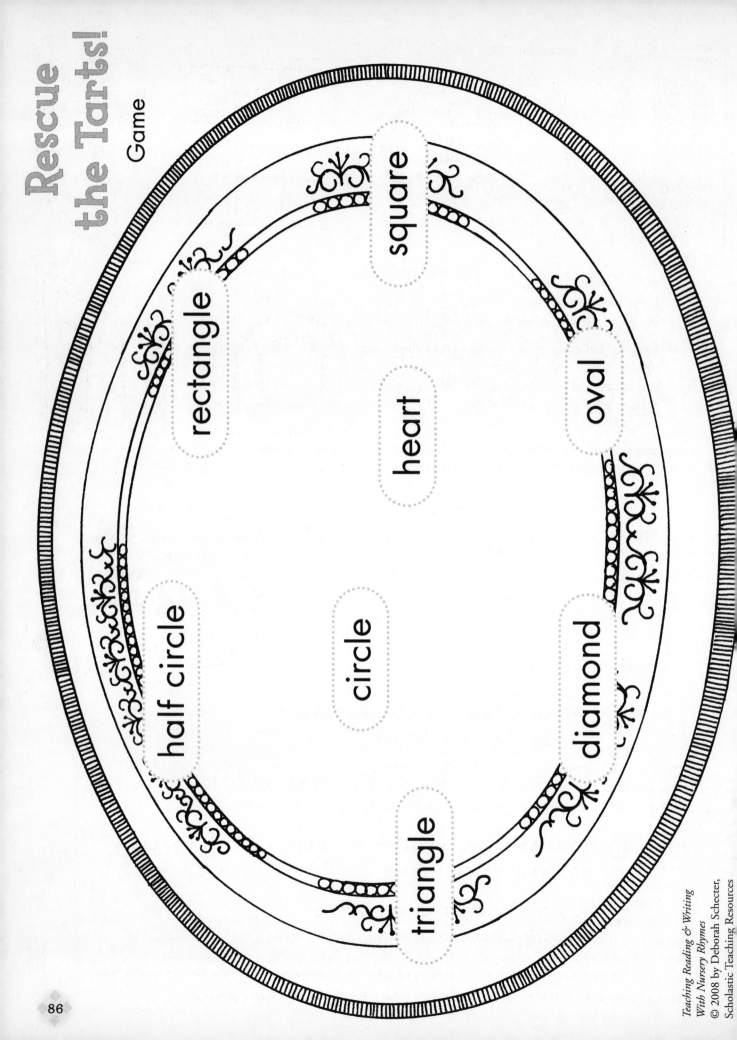

square

rectangle

heart

oval

half circle

circle

diamond

triangle

*Teaching Reading & Writing
With Nursery Rhymes*
© 2008 by Deborah Schecter,
Scholastic Teaching Resources

tart cards

Rescue the Tarts!

Players: 2

Game Directions

1. Take a card from the top of the stack.
   Name the shape of the tart.

2. Look for the word for that shape on your game board.
   Cover the word with the card.

3. If you have already covered that shape word, put the card
   on the bottom of the stack. Then the next player takes a turn.

4. Players take turns until both players
   have filled their plates with tarts.

made a
triangle tart.

1

made a
rectangle tart.

2

made a
square tart.

3

made a
circle tart.

4

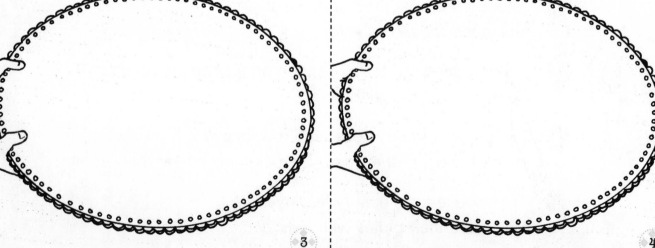

Teaching Reading & Writing With Nursery Rhymes © 2008 by Deborah Schecter, Scholastic Teaching Resources

made an

oval tart.

5

made a

diamond tart.

6

The Queen of Hearts made _____ tarts in all.

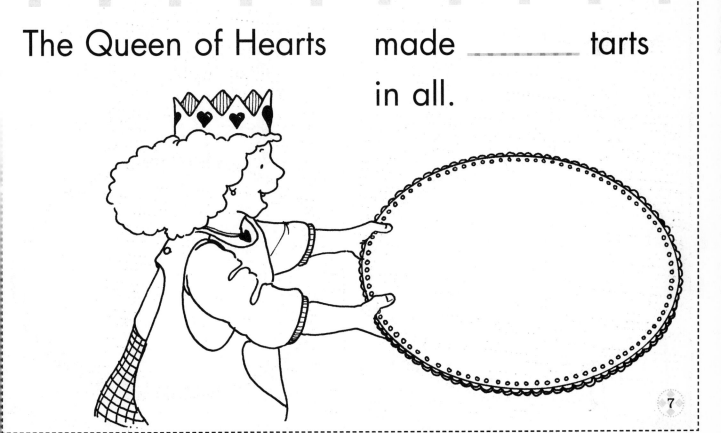

7

Teaching Reading & Writing With Nursery Rhymes © 2008 by Deborah Schecter, Scholastic Teaching Resources

Pease Porridge Hot

Pease porridge hot,
pease porridge cold,
pease porridge in the pot
nine days old.
Some like it hot,
some like it cold,
some like it in the pot
nine days old.

Teaching Reading & Writing With Nursery Rhymes © 2008 by Deborah Schecter, Scholastic Teaching Resources

Pease Porridge Hot

CONCEPTS & SKILLS

Vocabulary
◆ Opposites
◆ Names for foods around the world

Comprehension
◆ Text-to-self and text-to-world connections

Getting Ready

1. Write the poem (page 90) on sentence strips and place in a pocket chart. Or copy the page onto a transparency.

2. See page 7 for suggested ways to use the poetry page with your class.

Reading the Rhyme

1. Before reading the rhyme, discuss with children the kinds of cereal they like. Ask, "Which do you like best? Hot or cold cereal? What is your favorite?" (See Focus On... Comprehension and Vocabulary, page 93, for a related activity.)

2. Read aloud the rhyme. Ask children what they think *pease porridge* is. Explain that long ago, people cooked a thick food, similar to oatmeal and other hot cereals, made from peas. Point out the difference in spelling of the word *pease* (from Old English) with the modern spelling, *peas*.

3. Read the rhyme again, inviting children to clap their hands in rhythm with the words. On a third reading, have children clap and join you in reading.

4. Explain that long ago people cooked porridge in a pot that hung over a fire. They often ate it for breakfast, lunch, and dinner. Since there were no refrigerators, the leftovers stayed in the pot, sometimes for several days. Each night, the fire would go out and in the morning, they ate the porridge cold.

5. Highlight the word *hot* in the rhyme. Ask children if they can spot the word that means the opposite (*cold*).

6. Read the phrase "nine days old" and ask children if they can name the word that is the opposite of *old* (*new*). Ask: "When would the porridge be new?" (*when it was first made*) Brainstorm other pairs of opposites.

MATERIALS

★ pocket chart and sentence strips, or transparency and overhead projector

★ marker

★ self-sticking notes, different sizes

* pot patterns (pages 94–95)
* wooden craft spoons or spoon patterns (page 95)
* permanent marker
* crayons, colored pencils, or markers
* scissors
* craft knife (adult use only)
* My Nursery Rhyme Read-and-Write Sheet (page 16)

Teaching Tips

▲ ▲ ▲ ▲ ▲ ▲

◆ As an added challenge, leave the spoon patterns blank. Ask children to think of the words that mean the opposite of the ones on the pots and write them on the spoons.

◆ Extend the activity by having children cut out pictures from magazines that illustrate pairs of opposites and make word cards for them. Use the pictures and word cards to create an Opposites word wall. Encourage children to use the words on the word wall in their writing.

Porridge-Pot Opposites

Children practice recognizing words that are opposites by pairing up cooking spoons with their corresponding porridge pots.

Getting Ready

1. Make enough copies of the pot and spoon patterns (if using) so that there is a pot and spoon for every two children. On each pot and spoon pair, write a set of opposites (one word per pattern). For example, write the word *in* on the pot and the word *out* on a spoon. (For examples, see list, page 93.)

2. Color, laminate, and cut out the patterns. Cut a slit along the dotted line on each pot.

Introducing the Activity

1. Begin by letting children review pairs of words that are opposites. Choose a pot and spoon labeled with opposites (for example, a pot labeled *no* and a spoon labeled *yes*). Display the pot, read aloud the word *no* and ask children to tell you the opposite. Hold up the spoon labeled *yes* and insert it into the slit of the pot. Practice a few more to make sure that children understand how to do the activity.

2. Divide the class into two groups. Give the pots to children in one group and the spoons to children in the other. Explain to children that they will be pairing the pots with their corresponding spoons. To do this, children need to find the classmate holding the pot or spoon with a word on it that is the opposite of their word.

3. Let children roam the room reading the words on one another's pots and spoons, looking for their match.

4. When children make a match, have them slip the spoon into the pot and sit down. Afterward, let each pair of children read their words to the class and use each word in a sentence.

5. Remove the spoons from the pots, mix them up, and play again. (Give pots to children who had spoons, and spoons to children who had pots). Later, place the pots and spoons at a center for children to match up. Encourage children to write on their record sheets each pair of opposites they match.

Focus On . . .

Vocabulary: Opposites Array

Help children expand their vocabulary further by exploring words that describe the continuum between pairs of opposites.

1. Write each of the following words on separate index cards and then mix up the cards. (Use fewer words, if desired.)

   boiling, scalding, hot, warm, lukewarm, room temperature, cool, chilly, ice-cold, freezing

2. Review with children the words and their meanings. Then randomly hand out the cards. Tell children with cards to arrange themselves in a line so that their words are organized from the ones meaning the hottest to the coldest. Encourage children to compare and contrast the words and share ideas as they make their decisions.

3. Afterward, ask children with cards to explain why they placed themselves as they did. Did everyone always agree on where certain words should go? Why or why not? Invite the rest of the class to offer their ideas.

4. Later, create a How Hot? How Cold? word wall by drawing a large thermometer outline on craft paper. Write the words in step 1 on the thermometer by degree of temperature (hottest at the top to coldest at the bottom).

Comprehension and Vocabulary:
Text-to-Self and Text-to-World Connections

In the rhyme, pease porridge—hot or cold—is the only meal for days on end. Launch a discussion about different kinds of cereal. Say, "Porridge is one kind of cereal. What are some other kinds do you know?" List examples children name. You might sort the list into hot and cold cereals and then graph children's favorites. Since children are sure to name a variety of sweetened cereals, expand the discussion to talk about healthy food choices and the importance of eating foods made from whole grains. As an extension, help children research cereals eaten around the world, such as *rice congee* (China), *pohe* (India), *ugala* (Kenya), and *kasha* (Eastern Europe).

Opposites

in, out
come, go
give, take
before, after
always, never
to, from
no, yes
on, off
big, little
stop, start
above, below
buy, sell
empty, full
slow, fast
happy, sad
far, near
same, different
soft, hard
tall, short
top, bottom
weak, strong
wet, dry
win, lose
young, old
first, last
front, back
large, small
under, over
day, night
shiny, dull
rough, smooth

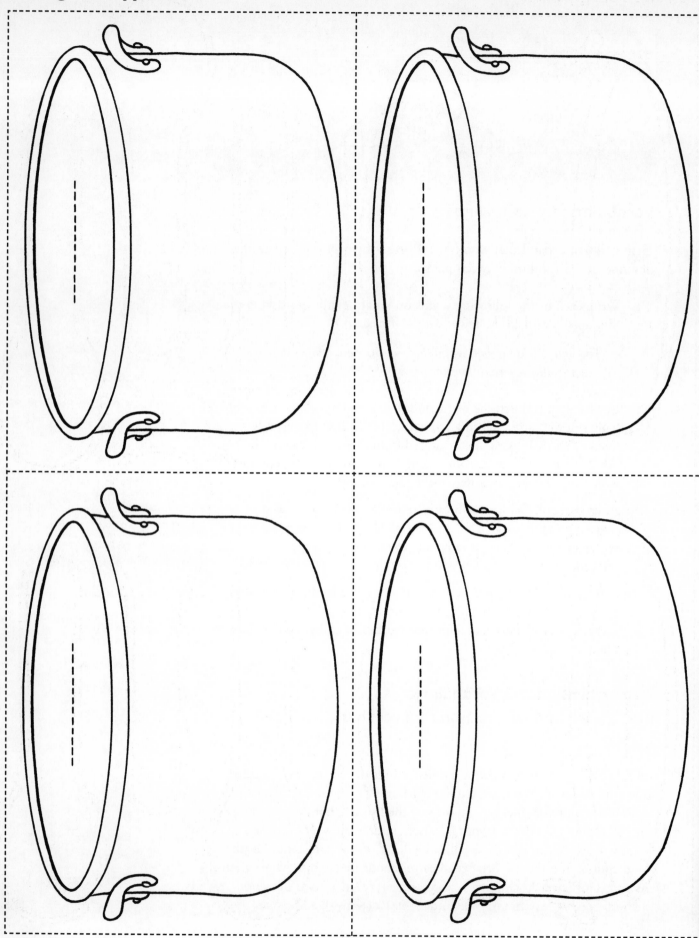

Porridge-Pot Opposites

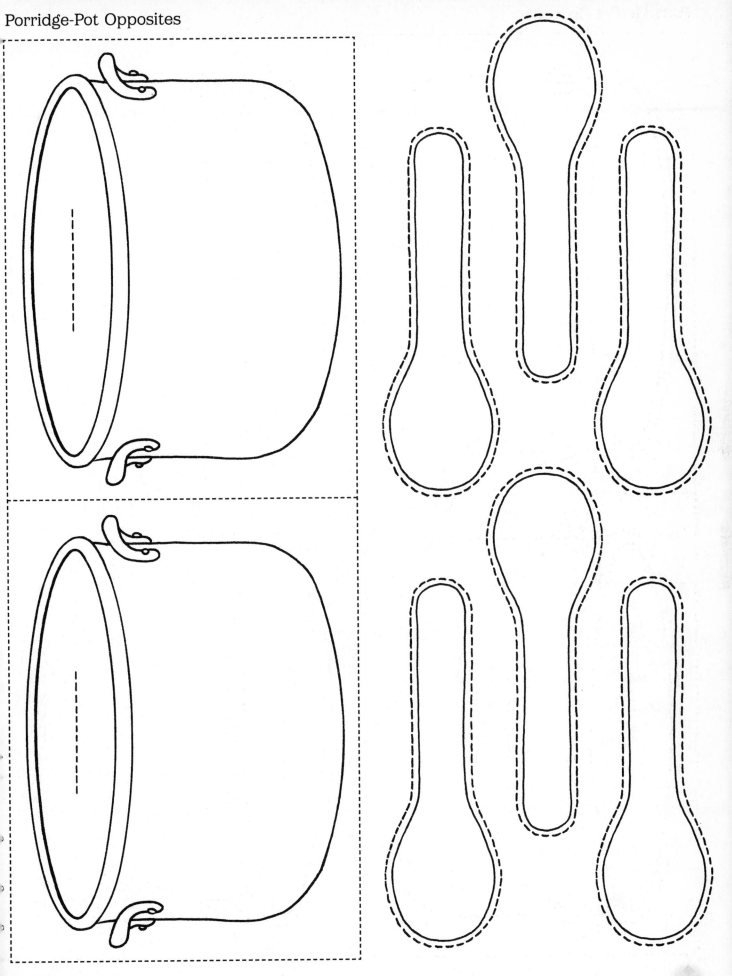

Roses Are Red

Roses are red.
Violets are blue.
Sugar is sweet
and so are you.

Teaching Reading & Writing With Nursery Rhymes © 2008 by Deborah Schecter, Scholastic Teaching Resources

Roses Are Red

CONCEPTS & SKILLS

Vocabulary and Writing
◆ Color words

Comprehension
◆ Text-to-world connections

Getting Ready

1. Write the poem (page 96) on sentence strips and place in a pocket chart.

2. See page 7 for suggested ways to use the poetry page with your class.

Reading the Rhyme

1. Read aloud the rhyme. Then invite children to read along with you as you track the print.

2. Reread it several times, replacing "are you" with "is _____," using a different child's name each time.

3. Read the first line again and ask, "What other things are red?" (*apples, cherries, fire engines, strawberries, ladybugs*) Record children's responses on self-sticking notes and use these to cover the word *roses*. Reread the rhyme using each new word.

4. Repeat this process with the second line of the poem and the word *violets*.

5. Extend the activity to include other colors and things associated with them. On chart paper or a whiteboard, write sentence frames as shown, and invite children to offer suggestions for completing them.

MATERIALS

★ pocket chart and sentence strips
★ marker
★ self-sticking notes

Teaching Tip

Inspire the poets in your class by sharing other poems about colors, such as "What Is Pink?" by Christina G. Rossetti, and the poems in Mary O'Neill's *Hailstones and Halibut Bones* (Doubleday, 1989), a poetic tribute to different colors that will delight and set the stage for children to write original poems about their favorite colors.

Lace-Up Color Hearts

MATERIALS

★ heart patterns
   (pages 100–101)

★ scissors

★ hole punch

★ yarn

★ glue or tape

★ colored wipe-off
   markers

★ paper towel

★ My Nursery Rhyme
   Read-and-Write
   Sheet (page 16)

Teaching Tips

▲ ▲ ▲ ▲ ▲

◆ Make the cards self-
   checking: Before
   laminating, write a
   number behind each
   color word. Write the
   same number behind its
   corresponding picture.

◆ Ask children to explain
   the reasoning for their
   matches. A child may
   associate pink with a
   favorite teddy bear or
   purple with a type of leaf.

◆ Find out whether any
   children are color blind
   before having them use
   the lace-up heart as this
   will affect their choices.

Children practice reading color words as they create unique lace-up designs.

Getting Ready

1. Copy the heart pattern pages onto sturdy white paper and laminate. Then cut them out.

2. Punch a hole through the circles beside each word and picture.

3. For each heart, cut a piece of yarn about two yards long. Tie a knot at one end. (To prevent the other end from fraying, wrap it with tape.)

Introducing the Activity

1. To begin, call out a color word, such as *yellow*, and have children give you examples of things that are yellow (*lemons, taxis, school buses*).

2. Demonstrate how to use the lace-up hearts. Have a volunteer point to the word *yellow* on the heart and read it aloud. Then have the child look at the pictures on the right and find a picture of something that is commonly associated with this color (*sun*). Let the child choose the appropriate color marker to color the picture.

3. Starting from the back of the heart, model how to thread the yarn through the hole beside the word *yellow*, bring the yarn across the heart, and insert the loose end through the hole beside the picture of the sun.

4. Repeat this process with the other color words and pictures. (For *white* and *black*, leave the snowman and top hat uncolored.) When all of the words and pictures have been matched and laced, admire with children the design that results.

5. Once children are familiar with the activity, place both hearts in a center for them to use independently or in pairs. Encourage children to write the color words they read on their record sheets.

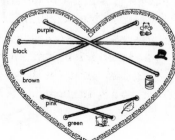
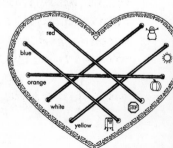

Focus On . . .

Comprehension and Writing: Color Words

Make Peacock Color Fans to give children practice writing and reading color words.

1. For each fan, copy the peacock and feather patterns (page 102) onto sturdy paper, enlarging them if possible. Cut them out.

2. Have children write on each feather the color words from this lesson, and then color the feathers accordingly.

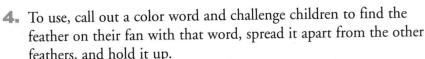
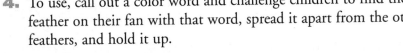

3. Help children punch holes in the feathers and peacock as indicated. Next they stack the feathers, place the peacock on top and secure using a brass fastener.

4. To use, call out a color word and challenge children to find the feather on their fan with that word, spread it apart from the other feathers, and hold it up.

Vocabulary: Shades-of-Color Words

Help children learn words for shades of different colors. Choose one color at a time to explore, for example, red. Invite children to find examples of different reds and the words used to describe these shades (such as *magenta, cherry, orange-red, ruby, crimson,* and *scarlet*). Have them collect samples from old magazines, clothing catalogs, paint-color sample cards, or sets of crayons or markers. Make a word wall with the color words and samples children find. For each color, draw and cut out the outline of a paint can from craft paper (in the corresponding color, if possible), and display. Fill each can with the color samples and words.

Teaching Tip
▲▲▲▲▲▲▲

Invite children to make fans for specific colors by writing or drawing on the feathers things commonly associated with that color.

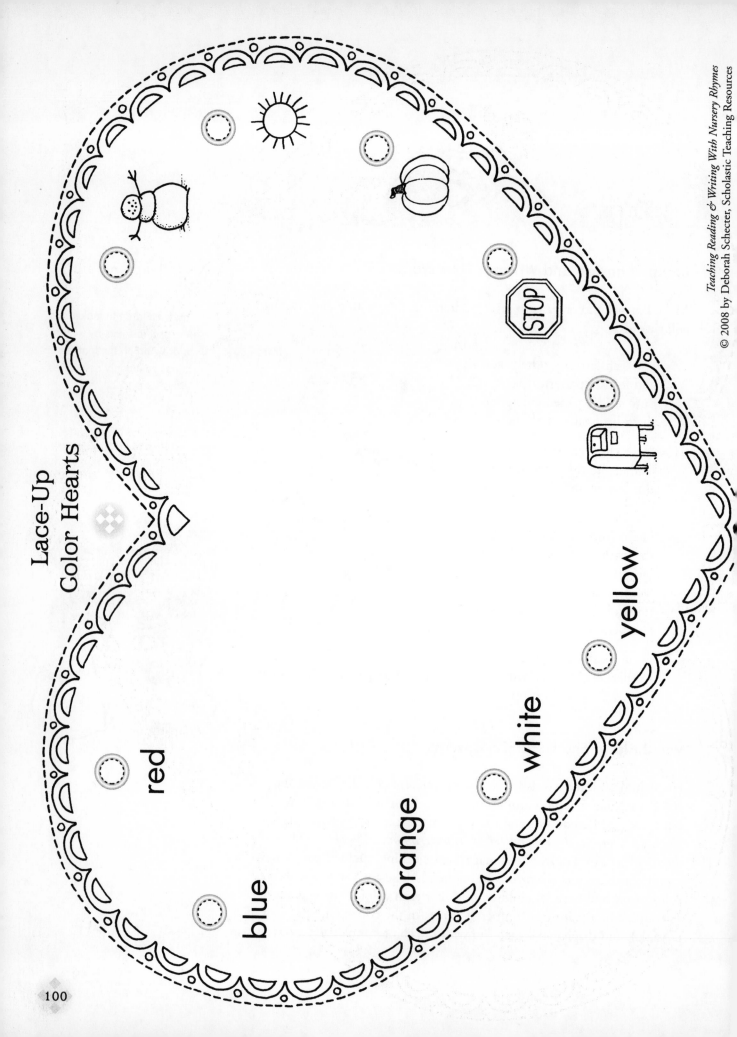

Lace-Up
Color Hearts

red

blue

orange

white

yellow

STOP

Color Hearts

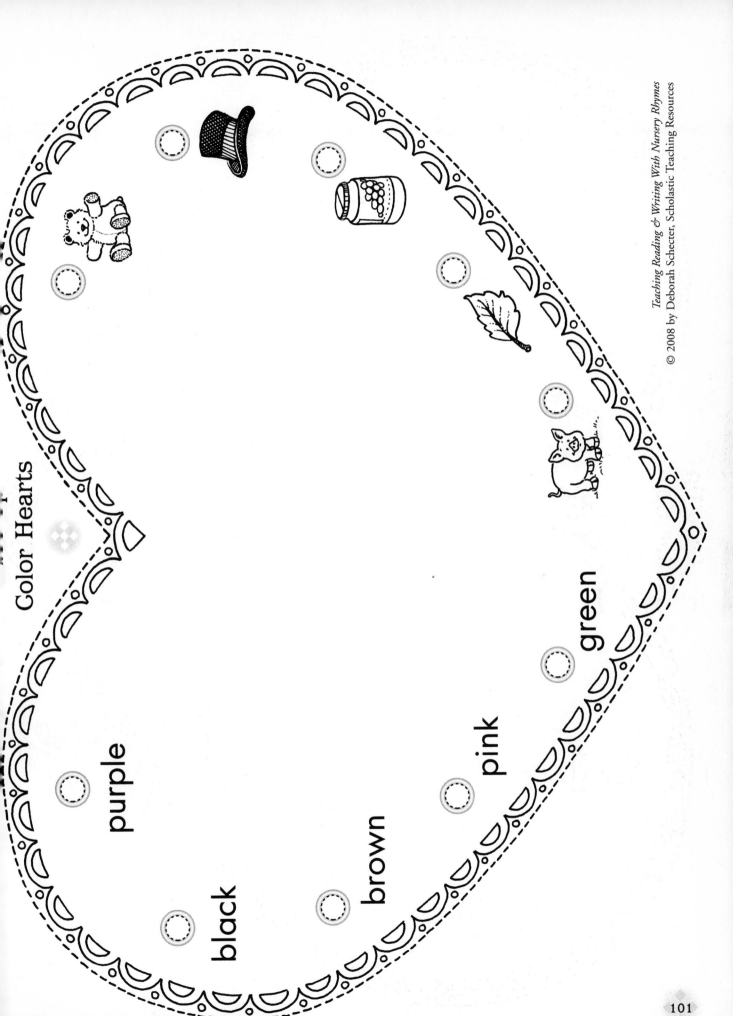

purple

black

brown

pink

green

Teaching Reading & Writing With Nursery Rhymes
© 2008 by Deborah Schecter, Scholastic Teaching Resources

Peacock Color Fans

Teaching Reading & Writing With Nursery
© 2008 by Deborah Sc
Scholastic Te
Re

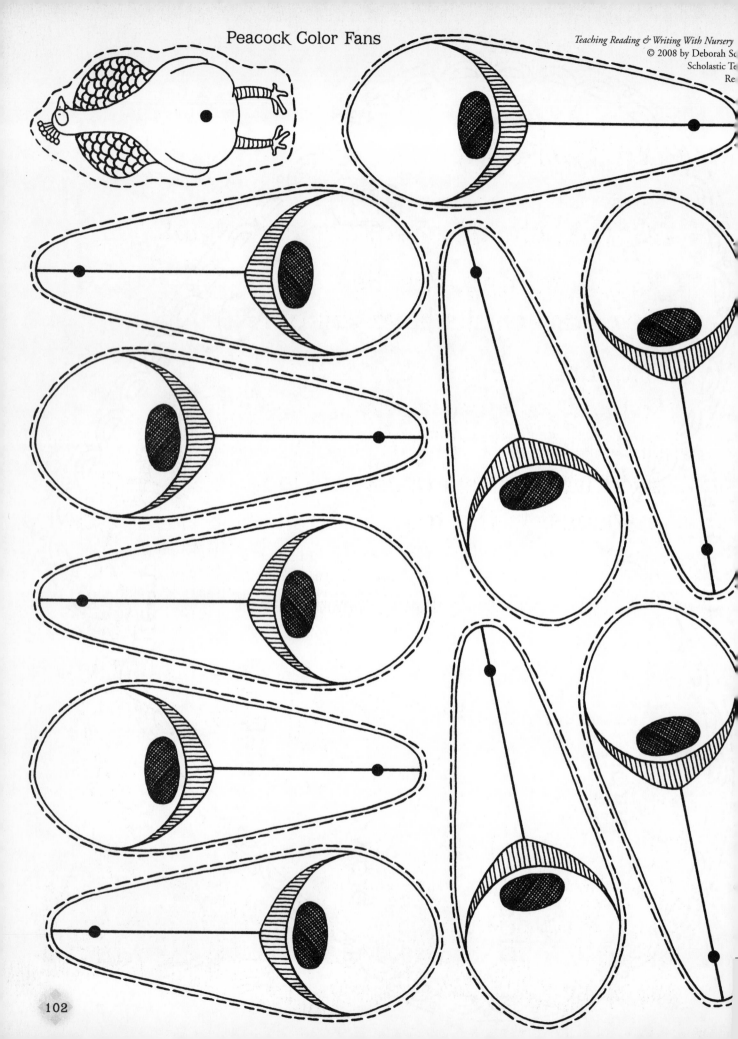

Mrs. Hen

"Chook, chook, chook, chook, chook."

"Good morning, Mrs. Hen.
How many chicks have you got?"

"Madam, I've got ten.
Four of them are yellow,
and four of them are brown,
and two of them are speckled,
the nicest in the town."

Concepts & Skills

Vocabulary and Writing
- Number and color words
- Describing words
- Responding to a prompt

Phonics
- Onomatopoeia
- r- and s-blends

Mrs. Hen

Materials

★ pocket chart and sentence strips

★ marker

★ scissors

★ chick patterns (page 107)

★ crayons, colored pencils, or markers

Teaching Tip

▲▲▲▲▲▲

To extend the lesson, write on sentence strips words for different patterns and adjectives (for example, *plaid, striped, fluffy*) and then cut apart the words. Color and decorate additional chicks accordingly. Then repeat the activity using the new words.

Getting Ready

1. Write the poem (page 103) on sentence strips and place in a pocket chart.

2. On extra sentence strips, write the word for each number from one to nine, and then cut apart the words. Also make a few cards for the word *is*. Place these at the bottom of the pocket chart.

3. On sturdy paper, make multiple copies of the chick patterns and cut them out. Color ten chicks as described in the rhyme and place at the bottom of the pocket chart. Also color extra yellow, brown, and speckled chicks. Set aside for step 3 of Reading the Rhyme (below), when children will innovate on the rhyme.

4. See page 7 for suggested ways to use the poetry page with your class.

Reading the Rhyme

1. As you read aloud the rhyme to children use your voice to show that Mrs. Hen is very proud indeed of her brood. Then invite children to join in as you reread it.

2. Ask children to point out the number words in the poem (*ten, four,* and *two*). Invite a volunteer to count out the correct number and color of chicks described in line 5 and place them in that pocket. Count the chicks together. Repeat this process for lines 6 and 7.

3. Ask, "What if Mrs. Hen's family of ten included five yellow chicks and two brown ones? How many speckled chicks would she have?" Use the chicks to help children figure out the answer (*three*).

4. Have a volunteer choose the word *five* and place it over the word *four* in line 5. Then let another child change the number of yellow chicks to reflect the new number.

5. Continue this process with lines 6 and 7, letting children place the correct number words and different colored chicks in the pockets. (If using the word *one*, cover *are* with *is*.)

6. Invite children to come up with different number combinations to insert in the poem.

Count-Up Chick Booklet

Children make chick prints to practice reading and writing number, color, and other describing words.

Getting Ready

1. Copy a set of booklet pages for each child.

2. Prepare shallow dishes of paint in a variety of colors, including yellow.

Introducing the Activity

1. Give each child a copy of the booklet pages. Also provide the other materials needed for the activity.

2. Have children cut apart the pages along the dotted lines. Then have them color and complete the cover, filling in the number of chicks in Mrs. Hen's brood (*ten*, or whatever number you wish to work with).

3. Review with children pages 2–4. Refer to the different groups of chicks described in the poem and ask children to think about the chicks that will be in their booklets. Explain that on each page they will fill in number words and color or other describing words for each group of chicks. Ask, "How many chicks will be in each group? What color or pattern will they be?" Then have them follow the directions (on the next page) to complete pages 2–4.

(continues)

MATERIALS

For each booklet:

★ booklet pages (pages 108–109)

★ scissors

★ cotton balls

★ tempera paints

★ thin markers

★ wiggle eyes (optional)

★ glue (optional)

Teaching Tip

▲ ▲ ▲ ▲ ▲ ▲

Let children use manipulatives in different colors to work out the number and color of chicks for their booklets. They can use crayons and scrap paper for other attributes.

- ⭐ Fill in the number and describing (color or other attribute) word for the first group of chicks.

- ⭐ Dip a cotton ball in the desired color of paint to print the chicks' bodies. Use a fingertip dipped in paint to make their heads.

- ⭐ When the paint is dry, draw feet, a beak, and eyes (or glue on wiggle eyes) for each chick. If children have decided to make yellow chicks that are striped or speckled, for example, they can use markers to add these features.

7. Guide children in putting their booklets together. First they place the pages in order behind the cover. Then they line up and staple together the tops of the pages. Invite children to share and read their booklets with classmates.

Focus On . . .

Phonics: Onomatopoeia

In this rhyme, Mrs. Hen goes "Chook, chook, chook . . ." Invite children to suggest the sound her chicks might make. In the United States, English speakers might say "peep" or "cheep." Ask children to name other sounds animals make (*meow, quack, moo*). Use this exercise to introduce onomatopoeia—words that mimic the sound they describe. List other examples, such as *buzz, plop, whoosh,* and *crunch*. Let children take turns reading the words, exaggerating the sounds as they read them. Start a word wall of onomatopoeic words. Tell children to keep an eye out when they read for other words to add to the wall.

Phonics: *r-* and *s-*blends

Use the words *brown* and *speckled* in this poem to explore other words that begin with *br* and *sp*. Write examples on enlarged copies of the chick patterns (page 107) and mix them up. Make two "nests" by filling plastic bowls or baskets with shredded paper and label each "br" or "sp." Place the materials in a center and invite children to sort the chicks into the correct nests based on their beginning letters.

Teaching Tip

▲ ▲ ▲ ▲ ▲

For more on animal sounds, see Teaching Tip, page 20.

Chick Patterns

Teaching Reading & Writing With Nursery Rhymes
© 2008 by Deborah Schecter, Scholastic Teaching Resources

"Good morning, Mrs. Hen.

How many chicks have you got?"

"Madam, I've got _____ ."

By _____

1

and _____ of them are _____ ,
the nicest in the town."

4

" _____ of them are _____ , **2**

and _____ of them are _____ , **3**

Humpty Dumpty

Humpty Dumpty sat on a wall.
Humpty Dumpty had a great fall.
All the king's horses
and all the king's men
couldn't put Humpty together again.

Teaching Reading & Writing With Nursery Rhymes © 2008 by Deborah Schecter, Scholastic Teaching Resource

Humpty Dumpty

CONCEPTS & SKILLS

Comprehension
- Retelling
- Problems and solutions
- Story structure

Writing
- Letter writing

Phonics
- Spelling patterns
- Rhyming words

Getting Ready

1. Write the poem (page 110) on sentence strips and place in a pocket chart. Or copy the page onto a transparency.

2. On chart paper, create a graphic organizer of an egg. Draw a large oval, divide it into three sections, and label "Beginning," "Middle," and "Ending," as shown.

3. See page 7 for suggested ways to use the poetry page with your class.

> Humpty Dumpty
> Beginning:
> Middle:
> Ending:

MATERIALS

- pocket chart and sentence strips, or transparency and overhead projector
- chart paper
- marker
- plastic egg

Reading the Rhyme

1. Read aloud the rhyme and invite children to join in as you reread it. Check for understanding by asking questions such as:

   - What happened to Humpty when he fell? Help children infer that because Humpty was an egg, he broke into pieces.
   - Was a wall a good place for an egg to sit? (To demonstrate how precarious this would be for an egg, let a volunteer try to balance a plastic egg on the edge of a desk or table.)
   - Who tried to help Humpty after he fell?
   - Why couldn't the king's horses and men put Humpty back together?

2. Reread the rhyme and invite children to make up simple hand motions to act it out. (For example, children might first make a fist to show Humpty when he is whole, then show him falling, and finally, spread out their fingers to show him breaking into pieces.)

3. Direct children's attention to the graphic organizer. Read the label of each section and explain that every story has a beginning, middle, and ending. The poem you are sharing tells a story—just a very short one! Guide children in reviewing the events in the poem and using this information to fill in the organizer. Keep the organizer on display so children can revisit it.

Humpty Dumpty
Beginning:
Humpty Dumpty was sitting on a wall.
Middle:
Humpty fell off the wall and broke.
Ending:
The king's horses and men tried to fix him but couldn't.

★ egg graphic
   organizer
   (page 114)
★ scissors
★ crayons, markers,
   colored pencils
★ construction paper
★ glue sticks

Teaching Tip

▲ ▲ ▲ ▲ ▲ ▲ ▲

Create a "How We Helped
Humpty Dumpty" bulletin
board display to showcase
children's work. First, tack
up a horizontal length of
brown craft paper at
children's eye level. Then
invite children to create
Humpty's wall by using
sponges and tempera paint
to stamp brick shapes in a
pattern across the paper.
When dry, arrange
children's egg pages so they
"sit" on the wall.

Help Humpty!
Problem-Solution Egg

Children use a graphic organizer to explore story structure and identify
problems and solutions.

Getting Ready

1. Photocopy the graphic organizer on page 114 for each child.

2. Cut out the egg pattern and then cut apart the top and bottom halves.

Introducing the Activity

1. Review with children the information on the egg graphic organizer made
   in Reading the Rhyme (page 111). Then focus on the ending. Poor
   Humpty! He had a big problem—he fell and broke apart. Was his
   problem solved? (*No—the King's horses and men tried, but they couldn't put
   him back together.*)

2. Ask children to suggest possible solutions—ways they might have tried
   to fix Humpty's problem. Record their ideas on chart paper (for
   example: *used glue or tape to put him back together, put him to bed so he
   could mend, called for help so he could be taken to the hospital*).

3. Give each child a top and bottom half of the egg. On the top half, ask
   children to write or draw a picture to tell about the main problem in
   the poem. On the bottom half, have them record their solution(s)—
   how they would help Humpty.

4. Tell children that since they have come up with ways to help Humpty,
   they can now put him back together. Hand out construction paper and
   glue sticks. Have children join the top and bottom halves of the egg by
   gluing them to a sheet of paper. Then encourage children to share their
   solutions with classmates.

Focus On . . .

Comprehension: Story Structure

To reinforce story structure concepts, give children drawing paper and crayons to illustrate what happens at the beginning, middle, and end of the rhyme. Afterward, invite children to share and talk about their pictures.

Writing: Letter Writing

Ask children to share about times they have taken a fall at recess or in PE. Explain that when we fall and get a scrape or bump, we usually don't need anything more than a bandage and soon feel better. But Humpty Dumpty took a big fall! Explain that sending a "get well" card or letter to someone who is sick or hurt is one way to cheer up that person. Invite children to make Get Better! letters for Humpty. Stock a center with brightly colored paper, crayons, markers, and craft materials (glitter glue, fabric scraps, ribbon). On chart paper or a whiteboard, brainstorm with children words and phrases they might want to use in writing their cards.

Phonics: Spelling Patterns

Help children explore the rhyming words in "Humpty Dumpty." Guide them to notice that *wall* and *fall* share the same spelling pattern, while *again* and *men* do not. Revisit other nursery rhymes. Notice rhyming words that have the same spelling pattern, as well as those that do not. Discuss how recognizing spelling patterns can help children read some words more quickly. For more practice, create the following center activity:

RHYMING WORD EGGS Write one word from a set of rhyming words on a self-adhesive label and affix to the outside of a plastic egg. Write rhyming words on slips of paper and place in a small basket. Repeat this process with two more eggs, using two other sets of rhyming words. Then set the eggs on a "wall." (Cut the bottom of an egg carton in half, the long way. Turn one half upside down and place the other half on top of it. Set an egg in every other cup.) Have children match the rhyming words with the correct egg and then put the slips of paper into it. For an extra challenge, use six eggs instead of three.

Help Humpty!
Problem-Solution
Egg

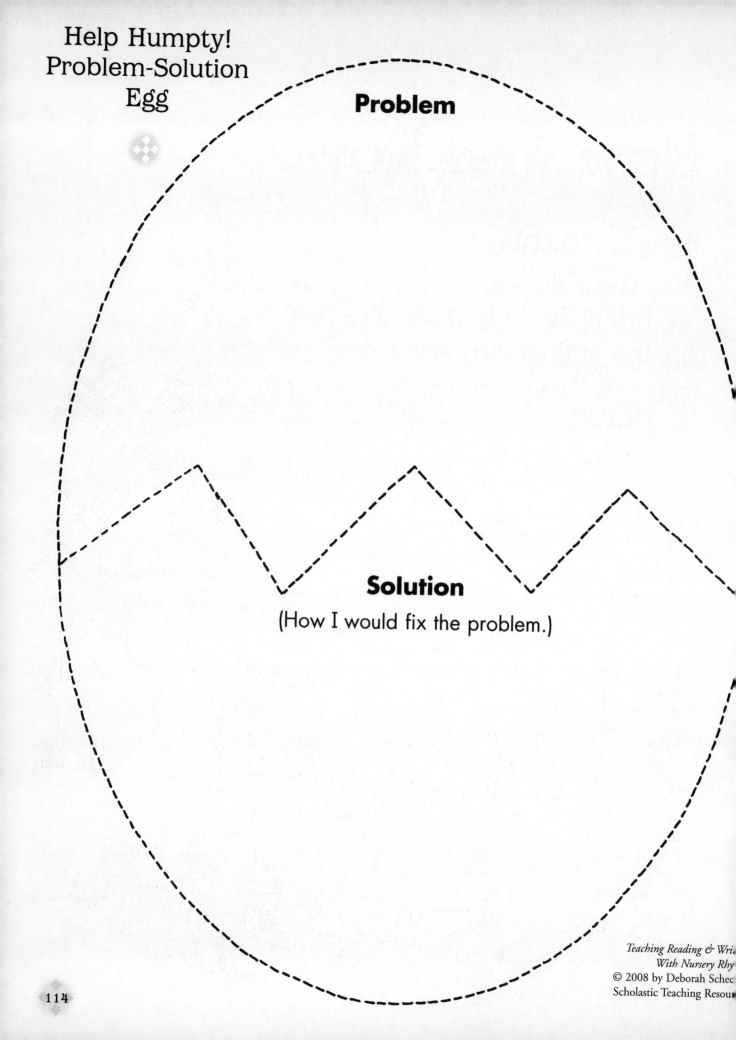

Problem

Solution

(How I would fix the problem.)

Blow, Wind, Blow

Blow, wind, blow!
And go, mill, go!
So the miller may grind his corn.
So the baker may take it,
and into bread make it,
and bring us a loaf in the morn.

*Teaching Reading & Writing
With Nursery Rhymes*
© 2008 by Deborah Schecter,
Scholastic Teaching Resources

CONCEPTS & SKILLS

Comprehension
- ◆ Sequencing
- ◆ Following a procedure
- ◆ Text-to-world connections

Vocabulary and Writing
- ◆ Descriptive language

Blow, Wind, Blow

MATERIALS

- ★ pocket chart and sentence strips
- ★ marker
- ★ popcorn kernels
- ★ cornmeal

Teaching Tips

- ◆ Show children a working windmill at www.golden windmill.org/videos/ videos.htm
- ◆ Show children how a windmill works by making a simple paper pinwheel. (See below.) Invite a child to blow on the pinwheel from the side to observe how moving air makes the wheel turn.

Getting Ready

1. Copy each line of the poem (page 115) onto separate sentence strips and place in a pocket chart.

2. See page 7 for suggested ways to use the poetry page with your class.

Reading the Rhyme

1. Before reading the poem, build background knowledge related to the topic of windmills. Begin by asking children what they know about the wind. How do they know when the wind is blowing hard? (*tree branches bend, flags wave, hats blow off people's heads*)

2. Explain that people can use the wind's power to help them do work. Ask, "Does anyone know what a windmill does?" Invite children to share what they know about how windmills work. If possible, show children photographs of windmills (see Teaching Tips, left.)

3. Read aloud the rhyme several times. Then ask, "Why is the wind so important in this poem?" Explain that the wind makes the sail-like blades on a windmill turn. As the blades turn, they create energy that makes it easier for people to do hard work.

4. Review the poem line by line. Explain that long ago people used a windmill's energy to help them grind (break into tiny pieces) the hard dry corn that people used to make bread. People who do the job of grinding corn into cornmeal are called millers.

Make a Pinwheel

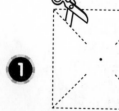

1 Cut out a 5-inch square of paper. Make four cuts as shown.

2 Bring every other corner into the center, one on top of another. Hold the corners in place with your finger.

3 Push a pushpin through the center. Then push the pin into the side of a pencil eraser.

5. Show children some popcorn kernels and some cornmeal. Invite them to describe how the corn is alike and different in each form (*both: yellow/golden color; dried popcorn: hard, bumpy; cornmeal: soft, powdery*).

6. Remove the sentence strips from the pocket chart, scramble them, and return them to the chart out of order. Then read aloud the poem. Children are sure to tell you that that the poem no longer rhymes or makes sense.

7. Ask for children's help in putting the sentence strips back in the correct order. What clues might children use? (*lines that end in the same rhyming sound, what steps need to come first, second, and so on*)

❖ Windmill Sequencing Book ❖

MATERIALS

★ mini-book and windmill blades patterns (pages 120–122)
★ scissors
★ paper clips
★ crayons or markers
★ brass fasteners
★ hole punch

To practice sequencing skills, children use text and picture context clues to put the pages of a mini-book in order.

Getting Ready

1. Make a class set of the mini-book pages on sturdy paper and cut them apart. Cut out the windmill blades pattern and set aside.

2. Scramble each set of mini-book pages (same scrambled order for each set) and secure with a paper clip.

Introducing the Activity

1. Divide the class into small groups. Provide each child with a set of mini-book pages and a brass fastener.

2. Read aloud the text on each of the mixed-up pages and talk about the pictures. What do children notice? (*The lines of the poem "Blow, Wind, Blow" are on separate pages and they are all mixed up; there is a blank box at the bottom of each page.*) Review with children your discussion of the poem and the steps in the process of bread making.

3. Explain to children that their job is to put the pages of the mini-book in order so that the story it tells makes sense. What clues might they use? Guide children to understand that they can use the pictures both to help them read the text on each page and to figure out the order in which the pages should go. Encourage children in each group to work together.

(continues)

117

Teaching Tip

▲▲▲▲▲▲

To reinforce the milling process described in the poem and add embellishment to the mini-books, provide each group with paper cups of popcorn kernels, yellow cornmeal, small pieces of cotton, yellow markers, small, thin rectangles cut from a yellow sponge, and glue. Guide children in following the instructions below to add kinesthetic details.

◆ **Page 2:** Glue popcorn kernels onto the ears of corn in the basket. For the ground corn, spread glue from the miller's basket to the top of the sack. Sprinkle with cornmeal. Let dry.

◆ **Page 3:** For the bread dough, glue a balled-up piece of cotton in the bowl. Dab with a yellow marker.

◆ **Page 4:** For the loaves of bread, glue yellow sponge rectangles to the baker's tray and to the loaf in his hands.

◆ Encourage children to compare the different textures beginning with the hard, dried corn, then the soft, powdery cornmeal, the squishy dough, and finally the spongy, fluffy bread.

4. Once everyone has finished, check that children's pages are ordered correctly, and then have them fill in the page numbers in the blank box on each page. Let children color their books as desired.

5. Give each child a windmill blades pattern. Help children punch a hole in the pattern and the mini-book cover as indicated. Attach the blades to the cover using a brass fastener.

6. To assemble their books, have children stack the pages in order and staple them together on the left side. Invite them to share their books with one another and have fun making their windmill blades turn. Then have children take their books home to share with family members.

Nonfiction Connection

✦✦

Help children learn more about the process of bread making and different kinds of bread eaten by people around the world. Suggested titles follow:

◆ *Bread, Bread, Bread* (Around the World series) by Ann Morris (HarperCollins, 1989).

◆ *Bread Comes to Life: A Garden of Wheat and a Loaf to Eat* by George Levenson (Ten Speed Press, 2004).

◆ *Grains to Bread* (How Things Are Made series) by Inez Snyder (Scholastic, 2005).

◆ *How Bread Is Made* by Neil Curtis (Lerner, 1992).

◆ *The Tortilla Factory* by Gary Paulsen (Voyager Books, 1998).

Focus On . . .

Comprehension: Sequencing and Following a Procedure

Make corn muffins! But first help children deconstruct a piece of procedural writing and also see the practical reasons for putting the steps of a process in order.

Make corn muffins! But first help children deconstruct a piece of procedural writing and also see the practical reasons for putting the steps of a process in order.

1. Photocopy the recipe (page 123) for each child and cut apart the six strips. Scramble each set and secure with a paper clip. Also make an enlarged copy of the recipe, cut it into strips, and place—in order—in a pocket chart.

2. Read aloud the title. Tell children that they will be baking corn muffins, but first they need to read and understand the recipe—the directions for making the muffins. Read aloud the steps as children follow along.

3. Deconstruct the text with children by asking questions such as:

   ★ "What does the title tell us?" Explain that it describes the topic or theme of this kind of writing—in this case, a recipe.

   ★ "How do we know what we need?" Guide children in identifying the various ingredients, using the picture clues.

   ★ "How do we know what to do?" Help children notice the key action words in each step, such as *stir, add,* and *pour.*

4. Mix up the strips, return them to the pockets, and reread the steps. Ask, "Does the recipe make sense? For example, does it make sense for the first step to be 'Third, pour into a greased mini-muffin pan'? Why not?" Discuss how the ordinal words and *next* and *last* provide sequencing clues. Then invite children to help rearrange the strips so that the recipe reads correctly.

5. Give each child a set of recipe strips. Remind children of the pocket chart activity they did earlier. Tell them that their job is to place the strips in the correct order. Encourage children to work together.

6. Once children have finished, ask them to read the steps, make any needed corrections, and then glue the rearranged strips to construction paper. Now it's time to make corn muffins!

Writing: Descriptive Language

While children are munching their muffins, help them build vocabulary. Ahead of time, draw a simple muffin pattern on a sheet of paper. Make yellow photocopies and cut out. Ask, "How does your muffin look, smell, feel, and taste?" Encourage children to use descriptive words such as *yellow, crumbly, spongy, fluffy, warm,* and *delicious.* Have children each record their observations on a muffin pattern and then compare and contrast them.

Safety Note

Check for food allergies before doing any food-related activities.

Teaching Tips

◆ While making the muffins, encourage children to describe how the batter looks and changes (*powdery, dry, lumpy, thick, wet*).

◆ Invite children to take home their recipes and make muffins with their families.

◆ After making the muffins, have children record the steps of the recipe using words and pictures.

Blow, wind, blow!
And go, mill, go!

Blow,
Wind,
Blow!

By _____

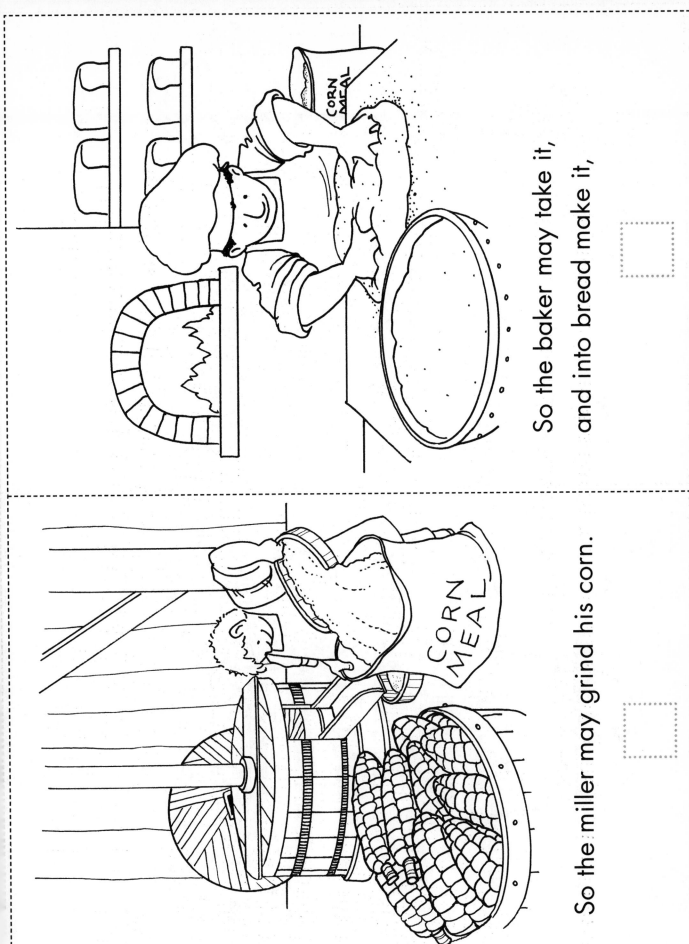

So the baker may take it,

and into bread make it,

So the miller may grind his corn.

Teaching Reading & Writing With Nursery Rhymes © 2008 by Deborah Schecter, Scholastic Teaching Resources

windmill blades pattern

Teaching Reading & Writing With Nursery Rhymes
© 2008 by Deborah Schecter, Scholastic Teaching Resources

Windmill Sequencing Book

and bring us a loaf in the morn.

How to Make Corn Muffins (makes 24 mini-muffins)

First: **Stir** together in a big bowl:

1 cup flour

1 cup cornmeal

$\frac{1}{4}$ cup sugar

2 teaspoons baking powder

$\frac{1}{2}$ teaspoon salt

Second: **Add** and **mix** just until smooth:

1 egg

1 cup milk

$\frac{1}{4}$ cup corn oil

Third: **Pour** into a greased,

mini-muffin pan.

Next: **Bake** for 15 minutes at 400°F.

Last: Let **cool**. Enjoy!

Little Miss Muffet

Little Miss Muffet
sat on a tuffet,
eating her curds and whey.
Along came a spider
who sat down beside her,
and frightened Miss Muffet away.

Little Miss Muffet

CONCEPTS & SKILLS

Comprehension
- Using context clues
- Point of view
- Predicting outcomes
- Following a procedure

Writing
- Using a graphic organizer
- Text-to-self connections
- Informational Writing

Getting Ready

1. Write the poem (page 124) on sentence strips and place in a pocket chart. Or copy the page onto a transparency.

2. See page 7 for suggested ways to use the poetry page with your class.

Reading the Rhyme

1. Read aloud the rhyme. On a second reading, stop at the word *tuffet* and ask children what they think this word means. Do a think aloud to model how they might figure this out: "What word might give me a hint? Oh, I know, *sat.* That must mean Miss Muffet was sitting on something." Then explain that a tuffet is an old-fashioned word for a low stool, usually topped with a soft cushion or pillow.

2. Continue, repeating the process in step 1 for the phrase *curds and whey*. Explain that this is a food, similar to cottage cheese, which was a treat for children to eat long ago. (See Focus On . . . Comprehension and Writing, page 127, for more.)

3. Read the poem again, this time inviting children to echo each line. Follow up with a discussion about children's thoughts and experiences with spiders and other creepy crawly bugs.

4. Expand on the poem by helping children explore the point of view of each character. Ask questions, such as those that follow, to guide the discussion. Record children's responses on chart paper or a whiteboard.

   ★ Do you think the spider frightened Miss Muffet on purpose or was Miss Muffet just afraid of spiders?

   ★ Why might the spider have come along? Because it wanted to scare Miss Muffet? Because it smelled food and was hungry?

   ★ How might the spider have felt—glad to have found the food? Scared of Miss Muffet?

MATERIALS

★ pocket chart and sentence strips, or transparency and overhead projector

★ marker

Teaching Tips

- For an activity that lets children practice predicting outcomes, see Focus On . . . Comprehension (page 127) before sharing the second verse of this rhyme.

- To help children learn about spiders, see Nonfiction Connection (page 61).

★ graphic organizer
(page 129)

❖ What Are They Thinking? ❖

Children explore point of view further using a graphic organizer.

Getting Ready

1. Copy the graphic organizer (page 129) onto a transparency for use with an overhead.

2. Make a copy of the graphic organizer for each child.

Introducing the Activity

1. Revisit the rhyme and review the discussion from step 4 of Reading the Rhyme (page 125).

2. Review the graphic organizer with children. Point out the thought balloons above each character's head. Explain that these are a signal to readers of what a character is thinking and feeling.

3. To help children practice distinguishing between the points of view of two different characters, use ideas from the discussion to fill in the thought balloon for each character. Repeat this process several times, using a variety of children's responses.

4. Give each child a copy of the organizer. Tell children to write (or draw) inside the thought balloon what they think Miss Muffet and the spider might be thinking or feeling.

5. When the pages are completed, invite children to share and compare their responses. Notice how many different interpretations and responses readers can have to the same text.

Focus On . . .

Comprehension: Predicting Outcomes

If children are not already familiar with this rhyme, mask the last two lines and read aloud just the first four lines. Let your voice trail off as you read "Along came a spider..." and then ask children what they think might happen next. Provide paper, pencils, and drawing supplies for children to record their ideas. Then finish reading the rhyme and ask children to compare their predictions with what really happened in the rhyme.

Comprehension and Writing:
Following a Procedure and Informational Writing

Give children practice in predicting, observing, and recording by making curds and whey.

1. Ahead of time, pour 1/2 cup milk and two tablespoons lemon juice into separate cups for children to share in small groups.

2. Explain to children that people long ago made cheese at home (and still do today) using soured milk. In this process, the milk separates into lumps or *curds*, and the watery liquid that remains is *whey*. Show children a container of yogurt or cottage cheese in which liquid (the whey) has risen to the top. The solid parts are the curds. During cheese-making time, curds and whey was a treat for children to eat.

3. Give each group a cup of the milk and the lemon juice. Give each child two spoons. Tell children to observe the milk and lemon juice. How does each look, smell, and taste? Let each child take a taste of each (using a fresh spoon for each taste). Record their observations on chart paper.

	Looks	Smells	Tastes
Milk	white	no smell like milk	good kind of sweet
Lemon Juice	yellow watery	funny sharp fresh	sour tingly icky

(*continues*)

MATERIALS

For each group:

★ small clear plastic cups

★ milk

★ lemon juice

★ container of yogurt or cottage cheese

★ chart paper

★ marker

★ spoons

★ data sheet (page 130)

Teaching Tip

▲▲▲▲▲▲▲

Borrow from the school cafeteria enough reusable spoons for each child to have three.

- Have children wash their hands before and after doing this activity.

- Check for possible food allergies ahead of time.

- Tell children to keep their hands away from their eyes because lemon juice can sting.

4. Ask children to predict: "What will happen when you add the lemon juice to the milk?" Have one child in each group pour the lemon juice into the cup of milk and stir. Let the cups sit for about 20 minutes.

5. After 20 minutes, ask children to describe what they see. (*Clumps of white solids—the curds—are on the bottom of the cup, the liquid on top is the whey.*)

6. Give each child a fresh spoon. Invite children to taste the curds and whey. Ask, "How did the lemon juice change the taste of the milk?" (*made it sour*) Give each child a data sheet. Have children use words and pictures to record information about their experiment (what they did and what they observed).

Writing: Text-to-Self Connections

Extend the rhyme by letting children write about their own fears and ways in which they deal with them. Write the sentence frames, below, on a sheet of paper and photocopy a class set. Have children fill in the frames and draw a picture. Later, invite children who would like to share to show and talk about their responses.

What Are They Thinking?

Name _____

What the Spider Is Thinking

What Miss Muffet Is Thinking

Teaching Reading & Writing With Nursery Rhymes © 2008 by Deborah Schecter, Scholastic Teaching Resources

Name _____

Date _____

Make Curds and Whey

What I Saw

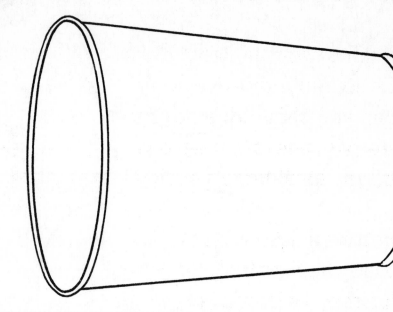

How did your curds and whey taste?

_____
_____
_____
_____
_____
_____

What We Did

_____
_____
_____
_____
_____

Three Little Kittens

Three little kittens
lost their mittens
and they began to cry,
"Oh, mother dear, we sadly fear
that we have lost our mittens!"

"You lost your mittens?
You naughty kittens!
Then you shall have no pie.
Mee-ow, mee-ow, mee-ow.
No, you shall have no pie."

The three little kittens
found their mittens,
And they began to cry,
"Oh, mother dear,
see here, see here,
we have found our mittens."

"You found your mittens?
You good little kittens.
Then you shall have some pie.
Purr-r, purr-r, purr-r.
Yes, you shall have some pie."

Three Little Kittens

Teaching Tip

▲▲▲▲▲▲

Use different colored highlighters to make the narration and the dialogue of the kittens and their mother distinct.

Getting Ready

1. Write the poem (page 131) on chart paper or copy the page onto a transparency.

2. Copy and enlarge two mitten patterns and cut them out. Color and decorate the mittens, giving each a different design or pattern, for example, bright pink with orange polka-dots, or green with blue stripes.

3. See page 7 for suggested ways to use the poetry page with your class.

Reading the Rhyme

1. Read the rhyme once, using somewhat exaggerated expression to make the tone and voices of the kittens and their mother distinct. Then ask:

   ★ Where do you think the kittens might have found their mittens?

   ★ Have you ever lost something at school? Did you find it? How?

2. Discuss ways children might go about finding a lost item. For example, they might retrace their steps; describe the item in detail to others, so that others can be on the lookout for it; or put up a sign with this information.

3. Reread the rhyme, one verse at a time, encouraging children to exaggerate their expression when the mother cat meows and purrs.

4. Read the rhyme a third time, inviting different children to read the narration and the dialogue of the kittens and their mother. Point out the quotation marks around sentences and phrases. Explain that these are clues that indicate when characters are speaking. (See Focus On... Fluency, page 134, for more.)

5. Show children one of the decorated mittens and tell them that a kitten has lost the other one. To help the kitten find it, they are going to create a sign that describes the missing mitten. Encourage children to use descriptive words to tell about the mitten (colors, designs, patterns, left- or right-hand). On chart paper or a whiteboard, record their ideas. Then repeat the activity using the second mitten.

Lost, Described...and Found!

Children help locate the kittens' missing articles of clothing using descriptive writing.

Getting Ready

1. Copy and enlarge the clothing pattern page. Make multiple copies and cut out the patterns. Also make a class set of the mini-poster.

2. Label a shoe box "Lost and Found."

Introducing the Activity

1. Tell children to pretend that the three little kittens have lost something, such a mitten, a scarf, or a hat. Then have each child choose a clothing pattern. Invite children to color and decorate their clothing pattern in a unique way.

2. Give each child a Lost! mini-poster to fill in for their item. On the lines, have them write the name of the item and then a description of it (noting its colors, patterns, textures, and other distinctive features). Tell children to put their name on the back of their paper.

3. Collect the decorated clothing patterns and place in the shoe box. Display the posters on a bulletin board at children's eye level.

4. Invite each child to choose an item from the Lost and Found box and then read the posters on the wall. Offer help as needed.

5. When children think they have found the poster that describes the item they picked, have them attach it to the poster with wall adhesive.

6. When all the matches have been made, review the posters together and invite children to share descriptive details that helped them make a match. Then remove the clothing patterns and place them back in the shoe box to repeat the activity.

Activity adapted from *Teaching With Favorite Mem Fox Books* by Pamela Chanko (Scholastic, 2005).

* clothing and mini-poster patterns (pages 136–137)
* shoe box
* scissors
* crayons, colored pencils, or markers
* decorating materials, such as glitter glue, ribbon, rickrack, pompoms, yarn, sequins, glue (optional)
* removable wall adhesive

Support for English Language Learners

▲▲▲▲▲▲▲

Readers Theater allows all children to participate and succeed. English Language Learners benefit from listening to the repeated readings of the text by other children. And as group members work together on fluency skills such as expression, intonation, and phrasing, they can offer each other feedback and encouragement.

Focus On . . .

Fluency: Intonation and Phrasing

The dialogue in this rhyme offers an opportunity to help children work on intonation and phrasing.

1. Review with children how quotation marks are used to indicate that someone is speaking. Then guide children to notice how ending punctuation affects expression and meaning. On chart paper or a whiteboard, write the same sentence three times, first using a period, then a question mark, and finally an exclamation point.

> "Oh, mother dear, we sadly fear that we have lost our mittens."
> "Oh, mother dear, we sadly fear that we have lost our mittens?"
> "Oh, mother dear, we sadly fear that we have lost our mittens!"

Read each sentence aloud and ask, "How did my voice change with each reading? How did this change the meaning?"

2. Have children work in groups of five to prepare a Readers Theater presentation of this rhyme. Give each child a copy of the poem (page 131). In each group, designate one child to be the narrator, three children to read the part of the kittens, and one to be their mother. Give children time to practice, paying attention to the good reading behaviors they reviewed with you. Encourage them to experiment with pitch, tone, and pace to make the poem's characters and their different emotions distinct. Ask questions to guide children in their thinking:

⭐ How might you make the kittens' voices sound different from their mother's voice?

⭐ How might you vary the kittens' tones to reflect their being upset at losing their mittens and later, their happiness at finding them?

⭐ How might you change the tone of the mother's voice in the second verse compared to the last one?

⭐ How might the narrator speak?

When a group feels confident with their reading, invite them to perform the rhyme for classmates. For added fun, provide props, such as mittens and paper-pie plates. Repeat the activity at another time, letting children switch parts.

Comprehension: Identifying Main Idea and Retelling

Share with children additional verses of the "Three Little Kittens" rhyme. (See below.) Guide them to identify the main idea of the poem: The kittens repeatedly do naughty things for which they are punished, but make up for their bad behavior each time. To reinforce this idea, divide the class into eight groups and give each a large paper mitten template. (Make these ahead of time.) Assign each group a different verse to retell through words and pictures. (Use the verses on page 131 and those listed below.) After depicting their verses on the mittens, have groups clip the mittens in order to a length of string tacked to a bulletin board. Invite each group to retell their section of the story. Wrap up by revisiting the main idea of the poem.

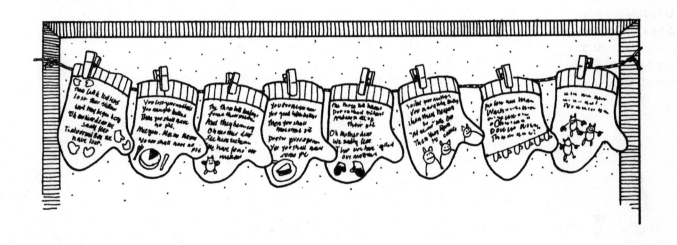

♦ Additional Verses ♦

The three little kittens
put on their mittens
and soon ate up the pie.
"Oh, mother dear,
we sadly fear
that we have soiled our mittens."

"Soiled your mittens?
You naughty kittens!"
And she began to sigh.
"Mee-ow, mee-ow, mee-ow."
And she began to sigh.

The three little kittens
washed their mittens
and hung them up to dry.
"Oh, mother dear,
do you not hear
that we have washed our mittens?"

"Washed your mittens!
Oh, you good little kittens.
Now you can play outside.
Purr-r, purr-r, purr-r.
Now you can play outside."

Clothing Patterns

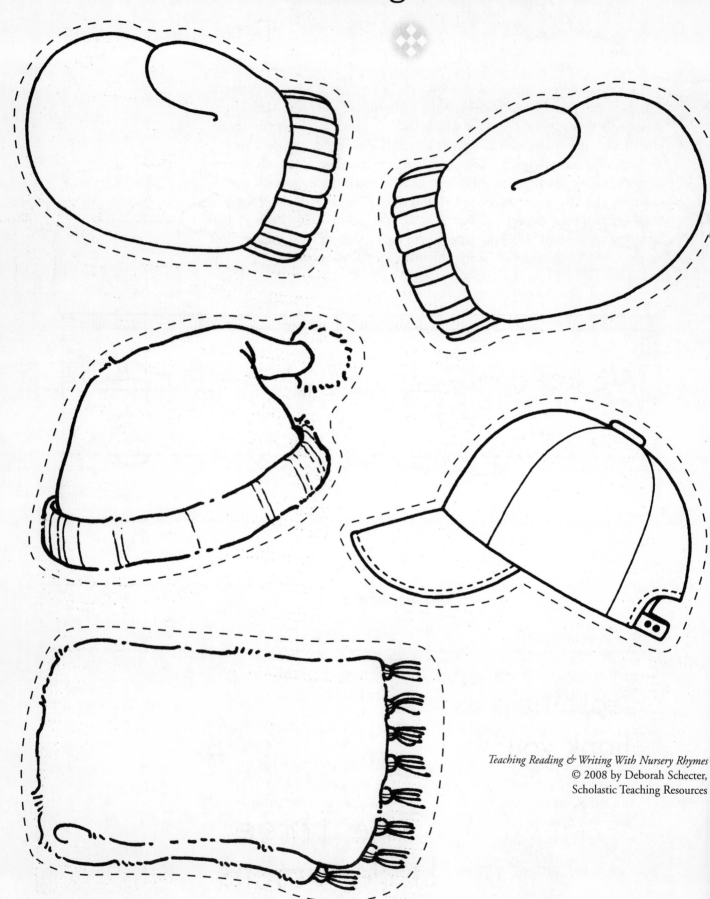

Teaching Reading & Writing With Nursery Rhymes
© 2008 by Deborah Schecter,
Scholastic Teaching Resources

Lost!

We lost one _____

_____

_____

_____

_____

Please help us find it!
Thank you.

The Three
Little Kittens

Old Mother Hubbard

Old Mother Hubbard went to the cupboard,
to give her poor dog a bone.
But when she got there, the cupboard was bare,
and so the poor dog had none.

She went to the baker's to buy him some bread,
and when she came back, the poor dog was fed.

She went to the hatter's to buy him a hat,
and when she came back, he was feeding the cat.

She went to the barber's to buy him a wig,
and when she came back, he was dancing a jig.

She went to the tailor's to buy him a coat,
and when she came back, he was riding a goat.

The dame made a curtsy.
the dog made a bow.
The dame said, "I am your servant,"
the dog said, "Bow-wow!"

Teaching Reading & Writing with Nursery Rhymes © 2000 by Deborah Schecter, Inc.

Old Mother Hubbard

CONCEPTS & SKILLS

Comprehension
- Fluency (automaticity, intonation, and expression)

Vocabulary
- Categorizing store items

Phonics
- Rhyming words
- Spelling patterns
- Long- and short-vowel sounds

Getting Ready

1. Write the poem (page 138) on chart paper. Or copy the page onto a transparency.

2. See page 7 for suggested ways to use the poetry page with your class.

Reading the Rhyme

1. Read aloud the rhyme with expression, stopping to discuss unfamiliar vocabulary such as *hatter* and *dame*.

2. Reread the rhyme and ask children to tell you what they notice about the lines of the poem. (*They rhyme.*) Ask children to point out words that make the lines rhyme, for example, *bread* and *fed*, and *hat* and *cat*. Circle these words and guide children to notice that rhyming words may have the same or different spelling patterns.

3. Invite children to join in on an echo reading of the poem. Read it line by line as children repeat it with the same expression, emphasis, and pacing. Read the poem several times until children become familiar with the predictable nature of each verse.

4. Let children take turns reading and acting out each verse. (One pair of children might read the verse while another pair acts out the part of the Old Mother Hubbard and her dog.) Children may also enjoy having Old Mother Hubbard visit other places and insert different rhyming word pairs. (See Additional Verses, below.)

MATERIALS

- chart paper or transparency and overhead projector
- marker

Additional Verses

She went to the butcher's to buy him a bone,
And when she came back, he was on the phone.

She went to the food store to buy him a snack,
And when she came back, he was packing a sack.

She went to the drug store to buy him cream for his feet,
And when she came back, he was eating a beet.

She went to the fruit store to buy him a peach,
And when she came back, he was making a speech.

She went to the baker's to buy him a roll,
And when she came back, he was taking a stroll.

She went to the shoe store to buy him some shoes,
And when she came back, he was taking a snooze.

More Mother Hubbard Adventures

Children build fluency by pairing up to practice reading and then performing other silly verses for this rhyme.

Getting Ready

1. Make enough copies of the verse strips so that there is one strip for each pair of children. (Use the sentence frame template on page 144 and the Additional Verses on page 139 to make additional strips.)

2. Copy the first and last verses of the original rhyme onto sentence strips.

Introducing the Activity

1. Tell children that they are going to practice reading additional verses for the poem and then perform them together as a class. Pair up children and give each pair one verse strip. Review with children their new verse, guiding them to use the picture clues to decode unfamiliar words.

2. Have children each choose one line of the verse and practice reading it aloud until they can read it smoothly. As children practice, encourage them to read at a suitable pace (not too fast or too slowly), pay attention to punctuation, use expression, speak loudly enough so the whole class will be able to hear them, and give each other feedback and encouragement. Allow children plenty of practice time.

3. Once everyone is familiar with their lines, bring the class together for a read aloud. Have pairs of children stand together in the order you would like them to read.

4. Place the first four lines of the original rhyme in the pocket chart, skip one or two pockets as a divider, and then insert the last four lines. Explain that everyone will read the beginning of the poem together. Each pair of children then reads their line of the verse, using their best performance voices. Everyone joins in to read the end together.

Teaching Tips

▲▲▲▲▲▲

◆ To assess comprehension, cut off the pictures from the verse strips, mix them up, and ask children to match them.

◆ Invite children to use the blank template (page 144) to make up their own verses. Give each child a strip to paste to a larger sheet of paper. Have children fill in the sentence frame and illustrate their new verse. Display children's work and invite everyone to read the new verses together.

Old Mother Hubbard

Old Mother Hubbard went to the cupboard
to give her poor dog a bone.
But when she got there, the cupboard was bare,
and so the poor dog had none.

The dame made a curtsy.
The dog made a bow.
The dame said, "I am your servant."
The dog said, "Bow-wow!"

Vocabulary: Categorizing Store Items

Create a word wall of items associated with each kind of store Old Mother Hubbard visited. On large sheets of paper, draw simple storefronts (or invite children to do this) and add labels (Fruit Store, Shoe Store, Toy Store, and so on). Tack the storefronts in a row on a bulletin board at children's eye level. Place a basket of blank index cards and markers beneath the board. Model how to use the display by encouraging children to name different kinds of toys, for example, *doll, video game,* and *teddy bear.* Label cards accordingly and tape them to that storefront. As children come across names of other items that go with the stores, invite them to create new cards for the display—writing the name for each item on a card and drawing a picture, if desired.

Phonics: Long- and Short-Vowel Sounds

"Old Mother Hubbard" offers lots of opportunities for children to explore words with long- and short-vowel sounds, for example, *old, coat, goat, dame, bread, fed,* and *hat.* Invite children to search the rhyme for words containing a specific long- or short-vowel sound. Then read aloud the rhyme and have children clap when they hear a word that contains, for example, the long-*o* or short-*a* sound.

She went to the fruit store to buy him a plum,

and when she came back, he was beating a drum.

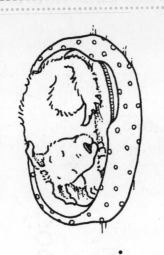

She went to the hat shop to buy him a cap,

and when she came back, he was taking a nap.

She went to the food store to buy him a ham,

and when she came back, he was eating some jam.

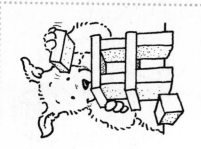

She went to the clothes store to buy him some socks,

and when she came back, he was playing with blocks.

She went to the food store to buy him some soup,

and when she came back, he was spinning a hoop.

She went to the toy store to buy him a toy,

and when she came back, he was jumping for joy.

She went to the baker's to buy him some pies,

and when she came back, he was trying on ties.

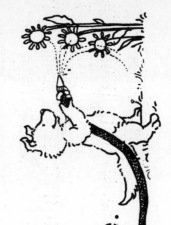

She went to the flower shop to buy him a rose,

and when she came back, he was using the hose.

She went to the _____ to buy him _____,

and when she came back, he was _____.